TEAM
POWER

Making Library Meetings Work

Barbara I. Dewey • **Sheila D. Creth**

American Library Association
CHICAGO AND LONDON 1993

Text and cover design by Mark Hoover and David Niergarth

Composed by Digital Graphics, Inc. in Linotype Sabon and Monotype Spectrum using TEX

Reproduction copy set on a Canon XBP-900

Printed on 50-pound Finch Opaque, a pH-neutral stock, and bound in 10-point C1S cover stock by IPC, St. Joseph, Michigan

The paper used in this publication meets the minimum requirements of American National Standard for Information Sciences—Permanence of Paper for Printed Library Materials, ANSI Z39.48—1984. ⊗

Library of Congress Cataloging-in-Publication Data

Dewey, Barbara I.
    Team power : making library meetings work / by Barbara I. Dewey and Sheila D. Creth.
        p.   cm.
    Includes bibliographical references and index.
    ISBN 0-8389-0616-8
    1. Library Meetings I. Creth, Sheila D. II. Title.
    Z678.83D48 1993
    025.1—dc20   93-1075

Printed in the United States of America.

97 96 95 94 93   5 4 3 2 1

CONTENTS

PREFACE

Library professionals are in an exciting and challenging period—a period in which every aspect of their profession and their library organizations will undergo considerable change. In this environment library professionals will need to acquire new knowledge and skills, to be able to exercise flexibility, and to make decisions in an effective and timely manner.

In this rapidly changing environment, in which computing technology, economics, and shifting needs of library users are creating tensions in all aspects of library operations, the library professional will need to be able to create new visions for information services and translate these visions into services. Library professionals will, more than ever, need to work together, within the individual organization and as a network of professionals across the country, to build collaborative work groups to solve problems and to design new systems and services. Decision-making in this period of constant change, accompanied by increasing demand for accountability, makes it imperative that library professionals develop their understanding of the process of communication and group decision-making and develop their skills and ability in working effectively within this new environment.

Decisions made within the library are often complex, costly, and visible to the public. They require library professionals to communicate efficiently and creatively with ever-increasing sophistication. Meetings represent the context within which a great deal of organizational communication occurs. As a critical aspect of organizational life, meetings should receive attention from professionals in order that skill and understanding can enhance the very process by which the library user is eventually served through quality ideas and decisions.

TEAM POWER: MAKING LIBRARY MEETINGS WORK provides a framework for library professionals to consider their environment and suggests ways to improve meetings as a central component of organizational effectiveness. Chapter 1, "Meetings, Productivity, and Innovation," reviews the purposes and goals of meetings as well as the challenges for reshaping library services in the context of productivity, innovation, and competition. Meetings are expensive for the library organization. The costs are largely in staff time to participate in meetings, but costs also occur with the inefficient processes and poor services that may result if the meeting context within which decisions are made is not effective at all levels of the organization. Because of the rapid pace of change and the increasing emphasis on productivity and innovation within the information service community, library professionals have to be able to increase productivity and respond innovatively to their users' needs while also reducing or containing costs. These dynamics suggest a need to create a greater reliance on clear and timely communication and the creation of organizational structures and processes that are more collaborative.

Chapter 2, "Effective Meetings: Basic Ingredients," discusses the meeting process and shows how time spent in meetings can be used constructively and creatively. Establishment of a different set of expectations and a commitment to change behavior for all participants can result in quality meetings. Participants and planners need to understand both the mechanics of meetings and the relationship aspects. The different types of meetings are described, and specific steps in meeting planning are reviewed, including whom to include, physical setups, and agenda preparation. Finally, strategies for conducting the meeting are presented.

Chapter 3, "Effective Communication in the Meeting Environment," provides an overview of communication theory and techniques that are fundamental to successful meetings of all types in all formats. Communications basics are covered, including aspects of effective interpersonal communication. Group dynamics and individual roles are explored in that meetings are essentially groups of individuals working together. Effective methods of group decision-making are reviewed.

Chapter 4, "Alternatives to Traditional Meetings: New Methods of Collaboration," examines computer-based networked environments now available for meetings of all sizes and for individual communication. These new meeting tools require a different way of looking at the communication and decision-making process. This chapter outlines the advantages and disadvantages of using these tools, such as electronic mail, telephone and voice mail, electronic meeting facilities, and video conferencing. It reviews the fundamental ways in which networked communications are changing the way librarians communicate with others both within and outside their institutions.

This book has focused on the belief that library professionals have both a need and a capacity to work more effectively through meetings to reach decisions and plan programs that provide improved information services for users. The meeting structure itself is no more than a collection of individuals. Successful translation of that format into quality relations and actions depends on the willingness of each participant to accept responsibility for the outcome of each and every meeting. Library professionals must be willing to develop a keen understanding of the dynamics of meetings, to invest time in planning and preparation for meetings, and to demonstrate willlingness to make the most of sophisticated communication and meeting technology. Far more important, though, will be the willingness of library professionals to change behaviors to create more collaborative and interactive relationships in order to meet the challenges ahead.

Meetings, Productivity, and Innovation

The fundamental unit of work in the modern organization is the group, not the individual. All groups incur coordination costs, defined as the time and money necessary to organize and sustain group activity. For instance, meetings must be scheduled, information must be shared, and individual contributions must be meshed.[1]

Meetings, meetings, meetings! They consume an enormous amount of time, both to attend and later to complain about. They seem as inevitable as death and taxes and are often viewed with as little enthusiasm. The issue of meetings and the problems and frustrations that they generate is a frequent topic among library professionals. Suggestions abound as to how to "fix" meetings, including dispensing with them altogether.

Why should meetings be worth attention by library professionals? What urgency exists in meetings, among all the issues and problems requiring their attention, that library professionals should devote effort to improving them? Several compelling reasons suggest that time spent on understanding the nature of meetings and how to effectively plan and conduct them is not only worthwhile to the individual and the library organization but essential.

Value of Meetings

Meetings, in some form, always have provided a fundamental way in which members of an organization achieve their work. Meetings come in all sizes and shapes and have a variety of purposes: the regular departmental staff meeting or management meeting; meetings of committees, task forces, or other advisory or planning groups that have specific responsibilities; external groups such as boards or trustees that review and advise. Some meetings involve individuals who work closely together and share goals while also understanding one another's responsibilities, personality, views— or so they think. Other meetings bring together individuals from different sectors of the organization where a cohesiveness based on shared experience and understanding does not exist. Indeed, such meetings may be comprised of individuals who are ignorant of one another's activities and contributions and, as a result, may occur in an environment in which distrust, even hostility, exists. And then there are meetings involving individuals outside the library organization. Such meetings may be conducted in a context of limited knowledge of and stereotypical attitudes toward librarians and the library or be serious political battlefields on which librarians must conduct successful skirmishes for financial and general community support.

Meeting Purposes and Goals

The purpose or goal of meetings varies considerably, from providing a forum in which information is shared to providing ones in which ideas will be generated, a problem addressed or a new service or product planned. Meetings may be held as well to address the more illusive goal of creating and maintaining a sense of commitment among a group of people who must rely on one another to accomplish operational activities or to implement a major project. In general, meetings as a vehicle for communication and collaboration can contribute in a significant way to achieving the mission and goals of the library by

- Keeping individuals informed and involved
- Promoting understanding, clarity, and commitment to the organization objectives, goals, and priorities

- Creating shared responsibility among organizational members for directions, priorities, and results
- Encouraging contributions of ideas, views, and opinions from a broad range of people
- Encouraging collaboration and team effort over individual priorities.

Most importantly, meetings should be used as a means to seek advice on a problem, an initiative, or an operational change; to encourage debate and airing of honest disagreement in order to reach the best understanding on any issue; and to achieve consensus and support for action. Meetings in their involvement of staff from all levels and sectors of the organization are able to contribute to short-term operational goals and strategic planning.

Meeting Problems and Frustrations

While meetings appear simple they are fraught, as are most group settings, with complexities that require considerable skill and understanding on the part of all participants to achieve the desired results. Therefore, it is not possible to define a formula for ensuring successful meetings, although it is possible to identify criteria for successful meetings, including the requirement to understand the dynamics of individual and group interaction. The goal, scope, content, and the personal dynamics of group interaction make conducting and participating in meetings one of the more demanding and frustrating activities in an organization.

Indeed, meetings are complained about possibly more than any other aspect of organizational life. Schrage states that "the reality is that most people *do* hate meetings. Most people are sickened by the mixture of boredom, frustration, and waste that comes with the daily/weekly/monthly meetings."[2] A study conducted in the corporate world in 1983 polled almost 500 management leaders regarding their views on meetings. Seventy percent said that meetings were a waste of time and 90 percent attributed meeting failure to lack of advance planning and organization.[3] A review of productivity at the NASA Langley Research Center identified meetings as one of the most significant issues affecting productivity:

The myriad of daily meetings surfaced as a recurring theme. Interviewees were not interested in eliminating meetings, but rather in focusing on ways to improve specific aspects of the meetings and to increase their efficiency. Typical comments about meetings were "too many," "wrong people attending," "start late/do not end on time," "hidden agendas," and "a perception that if you are not having numerous meetings, you are not managing."[4]

More generally, frustration with meetings can be placed in the following categories:

- Time required to attend
- Disruption to other responsibilities
- Lack of purpose or focus in meetings
- Poor organization in meetings
- Lack of results or action resulting from meetings
- Conflict between management and nonmanagement about issues and a process for decision-making
- Belief that meetings do not provide real opportunity for individual views to be heard; specifically that staff ideas are not accepted.

The reactions to meetings all too often are based on perceptions that, indeed, reflect an element of truth. Meetings are not likely to disappear, but will continue to be viewed as integral to organization life, which suggests that considerable improvements in the meeting process need to be made.

The compelling reasons for library professionals to turn their attention to the improvement of meetings as a basic organization tool include the cost of meetings and a more general need to address productivity issues; the pace and scope of change; the increasing competitiveness of information services; and emerging trends in organization structure and culture.

Productivity, Innovation, and Competition

Meetings cost organizations a great deal of money in staff time and energy. An estimate is that in corporate America, senior managers spend "seventeen hours a week racing from one meeting to the next, plus six hours preparing and who knows how many hours recuperating."[5] If even a small portion of this rather significant amount of time is wasted (and it is more likely to be a larger percentage of time), then the cost to an organization in lost productivity and poor quality products or services will be considerable.

There is every reason to believe that library professionals spend a similar amount of time in meetings. Time wasted in meetings, as opposed to the productive use of meeting time, represents first a direct cost to the library in hours and energy lost. Secondly, non-productive meetings may result in greater turmoil or low morale among library staff, clients, or administrators of the parent institution when poor decisions are made, the reasons for specific decisions are unclear or confusing, or implementation of major new services or systems are badly handled.

Aside from the direct cost of wasted time in meetings and resulting waste in operations when confusion exists regarding decisions, there is increasing pressure in all segments of the American economy to increase productivity. Snyder and Edwards presented a paper at the American Library Association annual meeting in July 1991, entitled "America in the 1990s: An Economy in Transition, a Society under Stress." They focused on productivity as a "crisis of historic scale and significance" facing the United States. They stated that "the only consistently effective means by which an individual or organization can improve productivity is to bring more and better information to bear on all types and levels of problem-solving, planning, designing and decision-making."[6] In order for this improved productivity to occur, more staff throughout an organization will need to be involved in contributing information, opinions, ideas, and assessment—and involved in meetings of one kind or another.

Kanter urges the avoidance of seeing productivity as purely a "mechanical issue of input and output," an approach that is often taken because it is "relatively easy to measure" but is a limited and limiting view. Kanter further states that this input and output definition of productivity results from "the confusion of efficiency with effectiveness. . . . And as Peter Drucker has long pointed out, efficiency is doing things right; effectiveness is doing the right things. And doing the wrong things less expensively is not much help." Kanter goes on to state that the

> Aspect of productivity that needs serious attention . . . is, rather, the capacity of the organization to satisfy customer needs most

fully with whatever resources it has at its disposal. This may require *modification* of product, development of entirely new products, or changes in the ways they are delivered. . . . [This] calls out for innovation—indeed for innovative thinking on every level of the organization's affairs. . . ."[7]

The importance of linking productivity with innovation is also made by Quinn and Gagnon in their *Harvard Business Review* article, "Will Services Follow Manufacturing into Decline." They stated that "too many service companies have . . . concentrated on cost-cutting efficiencies they can quantify, rather than on adding to their product's value by listening carefully and providing the services their customers genuinely want."[8]

Osborne, in his article entitled "Government That Means Business," focuses on the public sector and how tax-supported agencies (which, of course, include many libraries supported directly by tax dollars or indirectly through federal grants to the parent institution) must become more entrepreneurial and less bureaucratic. He states that voters don't want less government, they want "better government—and less expensive government. . . . They are frustrated with slow, unresponsive, inefficient bureaucracies that soak up ever more tax dollars and deliver ever poorer services." Osborne states that public institutions as well as private "must be flexible, adaptable and innovative. They must search constantly for new ways to improve services and heighten productivity."[9]

This coupling of productivity and innovation is essential within the library profession, particularly as the information "business" has emerged as a highly competitive environment in the past decade. Until the 1980s, libraries and library professionals were the primary organizations to collect, organize, and make available all types of information to all sectors of society with no charges to the individual user. This scenario has changed radically. Many different organizations and individuals offer what have previously been traditional library services, and they do so often with greater flexibility and timeliness than large bureaucratic libraries can. And many individuals and organizations seeking information are able and willing to pay fees for these information services. The competitive nature of information services, virtually unknown to most library professionals until recently, will be a reality in the future.

New approaches to services and new services are required to

ensure that library services will be valued in a rapidly changing information environment. The fast-paced environment requires that decision-making and the ability to capture the best ideas and to evaluate ideas critically be assured in all segments of the library organization. An organizational structure and processes in which staff are prepared to accept new approaches, methods, tools, and services, including dramatic changes over time in their assignments, roles, and skills, are necessary.

Creating a Collaborative Organization Culture

A challenge for library professionals is to create organization structures and processes that will encourage a far greater collaborative environment. A collaborative culture is more than one in which individuals are expected to cooperate and communicate; it is more than the cumulative effort of individuals. The collaborative environment encourages, indeed relies upon, individuals building on the ideas and efforts of one another, exchanging views and learning from one another, and through this process creating something that would otherwise not occur. In the collaborative environment individuals are encouraged and rewarded to do more than communicate but instead to establish a community within which ideas are generated and tested, not for individual gain or credit but for the good of the organization and its services.

Schrage says that "the act of collaboration is an act of shared creation and/or shared discovery." He also says that "if one truly believes that organizations succeed by profitably amplifying the talents of their workers, then the challenge is to create collaborative tools and environments. . . . [These] will become the sinews of organizational strength and personal development."[10]

Library professionals, using the available information technologies and personal expertise, are uniquely situated to create an environment to build collaborative communities. First, though, the traditional library organization structure and culture requires assessment in relation to meeting the multiplicity of challenges including managing the increasingly diverse published resources, responding to rising expectations among users for new services and faster delivery of services, and coping with shrinking financial resources.

Traditional Library Organization

The traditional organization of libraries has been structured around the functions of public and technical services. This divisional structure worked relatively well in the stable environment common to libraries until the middle to late 1960s. In this organization, activities are clustered based on similarity as well as access to manual files and materials needed to perform specific tasks. The traditional library organization created a vertical orientation with communication, authority, and assignments flowing downward through the organization and with essentially autonomous levels and units within levels.

This type of organization is referred to as *segmented*. It often results in barriers and divisions among staff that in turn generate both attitudes and ignorance that make it difficult for individuals to address effectively interdepartmental problems or projects. The segmented organization also limits the individual's understanding of how his or her activities support the overall mission of the library, and it further limits the effective use of staff talents and knowledge wherever they are needed across the organization.

Kanter describes the segmented organization as one in which only the "minimum number of exchanges takes place at the boundaries of segments; each slice is assumed to stand or fall rather independently of any other anyway, so why should they need to cooperate." Kanter further indicates that organizations where the segmented culture and structure dominate find it difficult to innovate or to handle change. She describes three reasons why this difficulty occurs: first, segmentalism discourages people from seeing problems—or if they do see them, from revealing this discovery to anyone else; second, motivation to find a solution to a problem is absent since people are encouraged to do what they are told and not think about improvements; and third, the biases and political conflicts of specialists tend to inhibit innovation since there is little incentive to consult with others.[11] The traditional library organization is a prime example of a segmented organization.

The traditional library organization is also functional in design. Drucker writes that the strength of the functional organization is the clarity and stability that it offers, and initially, a high degree of economy. But he goes on to state that the functional organization eventually becomes rigid, that the staff lack an overview of the organization, and internal inefficiency develops, requiring more and more managerial effort to make the operation run. In the functional organization, communication breaks down, and every manager "considers his function the most important one," which reduces cooperation and commitment to the total organization. And, finally, Drucker states, the functional organization is incompatible with innovating work.[12]

In the functional organization design, work is organized in stages and moved to the people with the skills and the tools to perform the work. This design, for example, is typical of technical services operations developed in the context of manual files. The outcome of a functional approach too often has the characteristics of an assembly line with all its attendant problems. While the work of public services is different in nature, there is seldom coordination among professionals in the medium to large libraries regarding quality or priorities for service. Departmental libraries and the many service departments in a general library tend to operate as separate fiefdoms with a structure that emphasizes vertical communication and exchange rather than horizontal or cross-divisional integration of objectives, ideas, services, and staff. Like the technical services work being moved to the staff with the tools and skills, the users in the traditional library have to come to the librarian at the reference desk who sits passively waiting to assist.

According to Drucker, the functional design works effectively in small organizations and in very stable environments, characteristics not to be found in many libraries whether academic, public, or special.[13] Change is the common denominator for most libraries and library professionals. In order to cope with the realities of change (including societal pressures), increasing complexity, and, most particularly, the demands of the emerging national online systems, library administrators began in the 1970s to implement a participatory management concept. Committees became far more prevalent in libraries, linking people across divisions and departments to contribute to decision-making and the quality of services and organization life.

While committees and task forces in the traditional library organization have contributed in substantial ways to decision-making and quality of life for staff, they are ultimately limited by the organization structure itself. If the library culture reinforces a value for the hierarchical and segmented structure, then the efforts of a committee comprised of people drawn from throughout the library system might be limited, with each individual protecting his or her own turf, or members being cautious in making recommendations that fly in the face of the established structure and processes or that challenge someone powerful in the hierarchy. There is often confusion among library staff regarding the scope and responsibility of a committee. Staff express a desire to have their views heard but when their recommendations are not accepted *in toto*, they are likely to feel that they are being ignored or manipulated. There is seldom substantive training to support individuals' understanding of how to accomplish work within the committee structure and, therefore, there is often a lack of understanding and experience with compromise and consensus building and an unawareness of financial and political realities that influence choices by administrators.

Administrators similarly become frustrated with committees and working groups because of what they view as a naive expectation that every recommendation can or should be accepted, as well as impatience with the amount of time spent on issues. While these frustrations can certainly be addressed to an extent within the traditional hierarchical organization, nonetheless the limitations of participatory management as expressed through committees and the like are partly due to staff trying to create a nonhierarchical process within the hierarchical structure. The old saying that a camel is an elephant designed by a committee reflects a perception that committees too often produce poor results; it also reflects the limitations on cooperative and collaborative efforts when bounded by the hierarchical organization.

There is a need to consider a model for organization design that integrates rather than segments work and people, and within which much greater collaboration is likely to emerge particularly through meetings.

New Organization Paradigm

Information technology is providing the motivation and the tools to consider a major restructuring of library organizations around a new paradigm. A centralized organization depending on manual files is no longer required, and the rapid access to organization information and communication through electronic systems suggest that the reliance strictly on a hierarchical structure also is unnecessary. The ultimate objective should be to shift to an organization philosophy and processes that will create intersections throughout the organization to accomplish work, to communicate information, to train and develop staff, to resolve problems, and to encourage collaboration in order to deliver the most effective and dynamic service possible in a timely manner.

What is required in the fast-paced information environment is a concept of the networked organization, one in which multiple relationships spanning departments and divisions evolve, and working relationships and work groups emerge based on horizontal connections. With a network construct relying on different alliances and work groups, staff resources will be tapped for creativity, energy, and enthusiasm, and frequent and multilayered interaction and collaboration will occur.

Kanter states that "integrative thinking that actively embraces change is more likely in companies whose cultures and structures are also integrative, encouraging the treatment of problems as 'wholes,' considering the wider implication of actions." Specifically, Kanter states that innovation flourishes in team-oriented environments. "Organizations that are change-oriented, then, will have a large number of integrative mechanisms encouraging fluidity of boundaries, the free flow of ideas, and the empowerment of people to act on new information."[14] The strengths of the team-based organization design, according to Drucker, are that it is receptive to new ideas and new ways of doing things, that there is great adaptability, and that it is the "best means available for overcoming functional insulation and parochialism."[15]

Peters indicates that the basic organizational building block should be the "modest-sized, task-oriented, semiautonomous, mainly self-managing team." He goes on to say with regard to teams, "train them; recruit on the basis of teamwork potential; pay them for performance; and clean up the bureaucracy around them. . . ."[16]

The team-based structure in a library could incorporate both temporary and permanent teams, as well as teams in which an individual would have a primary and a secondary assignment, or multiple "home-bases." The team design is based on bringing together people with a range of knowledge and skills to be applied toward specific activities or a project. According to Drucker, leadership is required within a team, not to give commands but to decide who has particular responsibility depending on the task; authority is task-derived and task-focused with the entire team responsible for results.[17]

In an article on team management, Hawkins outlines the following elements:

1. Team members share responsibility for the effective functioning of the group.
2. Power and decision-making authority is shared by team members, with the team manager relinquishing control to subordinates when appropriate.
3. There is a balance of focus on both task and social maintenance behaviors.
4. Task responsibilities may be redefined in response to changing task demands.
5. Freedom from restrictive programmed decision-making encourages creative forms of decision-making.
6. Communication is lateral and vertical, spans the boundaries of the organization, and consists mainly of information and advice (from the vertical channel), and of consultation (from the lateral channels).[18]

In an article describing the use of self-management teams in technical services at the Yale University Library, Lowell and Sullivan state:

> The benefits associated with self-management have already begun to be realized. Staff at all levels are actively engaged in problem solving and are contributing in new and different ways. Some teams are already aggressively pursuing change to work flow in order to operate more effectively. Morale appears to be at a high level; the general atmosphere within technical services is positive and upbeat. Perhaps most astounding is that productivity has already increased.[19]

In establishing self-managing teams at the Yale University Library, extensive training was provided to all staff, including special sessions for team leaders, to prepare them for this new environment.

The University of Iowa Libraries has been experimenting with the team concept since 1988. The first use of teams was in the collection development and management division, where thirty librarians were responsible for building and assessing collections and acting as liaisons with faculty in specific subjects. In 1988, three discipline-related teams of humanities, social sciences and sciences, and an international cluster were established. The primary focus was to provide a structure in which the librarians would determine how to share resources locally, avoid duplication of purchases, develop budget requests for the large number of subject lines in each discipline, conduct assessments of price increases, review decisions on electronic resources, and consult on various aspects of collection development and management.

The next use of teams occurred within the cataloging department, where teams similar to those established for the subject disciplines and for international materials were created. Since a number of librarians with cataloging responsibility also were involved in collection management activities, a link was established between both functions through the teams.

Finally, in 1990, a major reorganization occurred that expanded the team bases for library services. Subject divisions were established for humanities and social sciences and sciences, which brought together all staff involved in activities and services (whether public or technical) in one of the discipline divisions. Under this model, the humanities division is comprised of librarians who have responsibility for collections and faculty liaison, reference and user education, and cataloging as well as the support staff in the same operational units whose responsibilities relate to the subject division. Specifically, the humanities division brings together reference librarians and catalogers with responsibility for collections and faculty liaison in such fields as philosophy, English, religion, history, and linguistics with members of the humanities cataloging team (professional and support staff) and the art librarian and the music librarian.

The purpose in this reorientation of library structure and expectation for coordinated services focused on academic disciplines was threefold: first, to remove the artificial and dysfunctional barriers between public and technical services and instead promote all activities as service for the user; second, to provide a structure that should encourage, over time, greater collaboration among librarians in the delivery of services focused on one of the three disciplines, and to provide a base for better coordination of services in support of interdisciplinary academic programs; and, finally, to push decisions further down into the organization, encouraging lateral relationships and interactions rather than reliance on the hierarchy. The objective was to create a networked organization—networking the most critical resource, people—and one that would appropriately reflect the organization of the academic institution.

The team-based organization does require a different set of skills and attitudes among all professionals, including managers. Peters states that "one of the most dramatic requirements associated with increasing responsiveness is to shift the organization's entire 'way of being' from a 'vertical' (hierarchical) to a 'horizontal' (fast, cross-functional cooperation) orientation." He indicates that to accomplish this restructuring, the role of the middle manager must be reconceived as one of "facilitator and functional-boundary smasher, instead of expert and guardian of functional units."[20]

Specifically, managers need to rely on influence rather than authority vested in their position, to cultivate a commitment to cooperation and collaboration beyond what will benefit the individual or his or her department. They must work toward incorporating a sense of responsibility among individuals for the overall results of the team effort by using appropriate recognition and reward systems. Beyond the need for managers to change their orientation, the team setting requires all individuals to develop a high degree of self-discipline and responsibility toward activities and one another and to make the required effort to maintain clarity in communication and decision-making.

For a team approach to be successful, all members have to view themselves as having an essential contribution to make to the group. Individuals must feel welcome and connected to the group and not feel they are simply observers. Kanter describes four "inequalities" that can drive a wedge between individuals and the team. First, the "seductiveness of the hierarchy" may occur when people, "unaccustomed to the mixing and matching of an integrative culture, may end up duplicating the organizational hierarchy in miniature inside" the team. Kanter says that the seductiveness of the hierarchy has emotional roots, which are principally fear and comfort—fear of speaking out or "crossing" someone in power in the organization, and comfort in relying on the "familiar patterns of relationships and interactions."

A second inequality facing the team structure is that "participators are made, not born. . . . It takes knowledge and information to contribute effectively to task teams. . . ." Thus an inequality of access to information means that people will contribute differently to the group process. Third, there is the difficulty of "differential personal resources," the reality that people "bring to groups different levels of personal attractiveness, verbal skill, access to information-bearing networks, and interest in the task." Finally, Kanter describes the exclusionary process in teams when the "seniority/activity gap" exists. This gap refers to the very seniority of the team itself and the difficulty that newcomers have in becoming part of an already existing and highly active group.[21]

The reality of a team model has many challenges for professionals to learn new skills and different expectations for responsibility and working relationships, while it also offers the potential for greater organization innovation and personal development. Unquestionably, in the library whose organization structure draws on the team culture and values, professionals will find meetings with their requirements for open, frank communication and cooperation not a frustrating experience but simply a natural way to address policy issues, operational problems, and the identification of new services. The skills and abilities to operate effectively in a team structure are the same as those required for meetings to be a successful organization tool. In this environment, meetings are simply an extension of how work is accomplished—with coworkers and colleagues bringing individual ideas and capabilities together to address a common goal. Schrage sums it up best when he states that "the fundamental question is the fundamental challenge: In what ways can organizational meetings generate productive and profitable collaborations? The challenge is to meld the best of the individual with the best of the group in ways that are efficient, effective, and empowering. That challenge never goes away."[22] Schrage also believes that a major shift in the organization paradigm is the opportunity presented by electronic communication and communities.

Electronic Communication Systems and Meetings

Information technology and computer-based communication offer the greatest opportunities for creating innovations in library services and internal organization processes. In relation to meetings, electronic communication systems can go far to increase efficiency and, therefore, the productivity related to group efforts, and they can contribute to a distinctly different quality in interaction among staff.

Sproull and Kiesler state that

> Electronic group mail can decrease group coordination costs. . . . The scheduling constraints of getting everyone into the same room at the same time vanish. Because electronic mail is asynchronous, everyone can "talk" at his or her convenience; everyone can "listen" at his or her convenience. . . . Electronic mail . . . can approximate real-time interaction. Because electronic mail can archive the complete text of every message, the same group memory is available to every member.

They further state that in their research they "discovered a very high correlation between use of electronic mail and group productivity. . . ."[23]

Electronic communication, which is becoming increasingly commonplace in libraries, should be actively encouraged and explored to facilitate the various tasks related to meetings, such as scheduling, task assignments, and status reports, and for general discussion of topics and for generating ideas. It does not replace entirely the need for face-to-face meetings, but it can complement them by qualitatively improving such gatherings while also decreasing the amount of time spent on the housekeeping or managing aspects of meetings. In addition, as Sproull and Kiesler point out, electronic communication can go beyond the improvement of communication for existing groups and "more significantly, it can support groups and group activities that would be impossible and unimaginable without electronic group communication."[24]

Schrage sees the opportunities for electronic communication as providing a distinct departure from the limitations of traditional meetings, offering instead a format that "reinforces the idea that the meeting is a genuine act of creation." He indicates that this reinforcement occurs because electronic interaction "transforms the traditional meeting ecology—to discuss a topic, come to a conclusion, or make a decision—into an act of shared creation."[25]

Electronic communication, whether to a group or one-to-one, is the most important tool available to allow the organization to respond in a more timely fashion to library users' specific and immediate needs as well as to encourage collaboration that will lead to new products, services, and directions for emerging needs. The increased use of this form of communication will need to be actively encouraged within library organizations, through allocation of funding to provide access to necessary personal computers and communication software as well as through training in the use of this new communication medium. The topic of electronic communication is explored in greater detail in Chapter 4.

The availability of computer and software technologies also offers other opportunities for addressing what Kanter refers to as the organization's "capacity" to meet customer needs more fully. If the definition of a meeting encompasses any discussion or interaction involved with instructing, learning, resolving, and discovering, then there are many ways in which the new technologies can improve the quality of meetings, both for staff and users. Specifically, the use of electronic communication to offer traditional services online, as well as the use of hypermedia and expert systems, can provide new ways of reaching large numbers of users in physically dispersed locations and at hours that are not restricted to when the library is open. These new technologies provide the means to become a "library without walls" by instructing users and connecting them to traditional library resources and additionally to those that are online rather than housed in a physical facility.

The Online Environment and User Services

A number of meetings conducted by library professionals are often overlooked because they take place with one or more users as a part of a range of reference services. And yet it is important that professionals in every segment of library activities seek ways to improve the quality of these interactions, particularly making use of computer-based communication systems and software. The online environment offers ways to bring some of the same techniques used in the standard "business" setting to improve the quality and timeliness of delivering information services.

It is not uncommon for librarians to offer traditional services such as reference and research support using online communication networks. Library users are able to ask questions regarding a particular piece of material or a broad research topic via the network without having to phone or come to the library building. They are able to receive a response that is not only timely but that has permitted the person with the greatest expertise to respond to the question and also allowed sufficient time to provide the level of detail required. In addition, an online query can be forwarded quickly, a distinct improvement for a complex question over the current situation in which assistance is provided by the person scheduled at the reference desk, whose subject strength may well not be related to the topic being researched. Also in the networked information environment, the librarian can enhance the assistance provided to a local patron by using telecommunication to contact colleagues within the institution or even nationally to respond to a particularly complex research question.

In many library settings there is an increased need to focus on the teaching of users in groups as well as one by one. Specifically, academic librarians need to consider how electronic communication systems—text and video—will allow them to improve and enhance services for students. For instance, a librarian might develop an electronic conference system for specific classes in which large numbers of students are registered. She would be able to instruct students about resources for class assignments throughout the semester, without using time in the classroom, without working with each of the students separately, or without getting all of the students to come to a session scheduled in the library itself. A conference system also allows students to learn from one another and allows the librarian to avoid repeating information. It also provides a record for those who want to go back and review information on a particular question or topic. In this scenario, the librarian, working with a faculty member, assumes a dynamic role in teaching students about information resources by integrating them into the course-related focus, which should make them more meaningful. This method is an ongoing meeting with students that is being conducted online.

Academic librarians should use the electronic communication systems to meet more frequently with faculty and to stay current in developments and trends in the subject fields for which they have primary responsibility. In addition to the traditional contact with faculty, librarians might also join the electronic conference systems that exist for many researchers. For example, humanities librarians could participate in Humanist, while librarians working with physicists or chemists should consider joining the electronic conference systems available in those fields. A librarian might be an observer or a participant, depending on the topic of discussion and his or her ability to contribute to the discussion in this continuous meeting.

Equally important is the opportunity with these systems for the librarian to learn about developments in a timely manner and to understand more fully how researchers are sharing information and developments in their research. Academic librarians also might establish for faculty in a particular department or field a library conference system or bulletin board that would give up-to-date information on published materials that have been received, availability of electronic publications, or a host of other helpful information.

What is most crucial is that library professionals explore alternative ways to communicate and reach library users beyond the reference desk as the exclusive focus for interaction and assistance. Many other ideas and models should surface once we release the existing paradigm as the primary way that service can be effectively delivered.

Hypermedia Tools and Instruction

The development of hypermedia programs to provide basic orientation to library collections and services for users, while not commonplace, is no longer unique. These computer-based programs are usually developed by a team of library staff working together to define content as well as the structure of the program. An example of such programs is the *Library Navigator* developed at the University of Iowa Libraries by a team of librarians and a design specialist. The *Navigator* offers an introduction to the library system and to the main library, covering collections, policies, services, and physical layout. The library professionals are now working with professionals from the academic computing center to develop a program that will expand the *Navigator* to provide more in-depth assistance in the use of specific resources in the collection. The engineering librarian at the University of Iowa also is developing a hypercard program to provide reference assistance when a librarian is not available, guiding library users through the process of exploring resources in support of a research project.

A number of other libraries have developed similar software programs to supplement direct staff interface with users. Stanford University Libraries and New York University Library both have such programs, as does the University of California, Los Angeles. All of these systems offer new ways to provide guidance and assistance replacing or supplementing the one-on-one or group instructional meetings that librarians traditionally hold with library users.

While these orientation programs for users can also be used for orienting new staff who have little or no experience in libraries, hypercard programs have also been designed specifically for staff training. These programs again require cooperation among librarians and individuals with computer-assisted design experience to create effective educational tools. The University of Tennessee staff developed a program entitled "New Horizons in Library Training," a self-directed training program using hypercard. This project was supported in part by the U.S. Department of Education and Apple Computers, Inc. and offers an orientation for new library system staff by providing an introduction through seven topical sessions. Such software and individually conducted orientation sessions can improve the quality of training and increase efficiency by avoiding individual sessions in all situations.

Expert Systems as User Interface

Equally exciting is the potential for the use of "expert systems" in libraries to complement reference and instructional services. Riggs, in "Productivity Increases in Public Services: Are Expert Systems the Answer?" indicates that expert systems, a subset of artificial intelligence, require

> Programming vast amounts of knowledge into the computer to provide the basis for its "thinking" abilities. If library expert systems are to function like a human expert, then they must be able to do things human expert systems do. They must be able to ask questions, solve problems, explain their reasoning and justify their conclusions.[26]

Riggs indicates that expert systems in libraries are being applied in various operations, such as cataloging, indexing, management, reference, and bibliographic instruction. His examples include the

National Agricultural Library program, Answerman, that was designed to answer ready-reference questions. Riggs suggests that the complaints of burn-out, boredom, and frustration voiced by reference librarians due to the growth in demand on reference services, too few librarians to provide this service, and the repetitive nature of many questions can be addressed with the development of expert systems while also improving the quality of the service offered.

Riggs goes on to state that the use of expert systems "would improve the productivity of librarians by using their time in more constructive ways."[27] In addition, Riggs considers that library service can be enhanced if users no longer have to come to one or two locations for assistance and that assistance may be sought when the library is actually closed. These systems suggest movement toward a ubiquitous reference and instruction service and one that more nearly delivers service when the patron actually requires assistance; service tailored to the user, not the user tailored to the service. Riggs concludes by stating that "expert systems are not going to dramatically change libraries, but they are going to improve productivity and overall service."[28]

All of these computer-based approaches, and others that are emerging, offer enhanced means for meetings (dialogue, instruction, debate, resolution, innovation) among library staff and between library professionals and their user community. There is another more traditional vehicle for conducting meetings other than the face-to-face session: the telephone conference call. Technological advances have increased the usefulness of telephone conferencing, and professionals even in small libraries can take advantage of this form of telecommunications in several ways.

For a meeting of five or seven people, the long-distance operator can set up a conference call, dialing each person in turn until everyone is on the line. A speaker telephone permits several persons in one office to talk to a person in another office without the need for complicated equipment. Teleconferencing can occur among individuals in the same building or in separate geographic locations. In some cases, teleconferencing allows individuals to discuss and resolve an issue quickly without having to leave their office, minimizing the disruption to their work. Other advantages include

Basic technology—the telephone—is owned by everyone.

People can meet who otherwise might not be able to because of time and cost factors.

Conversation is usually focused because people cannot see one another, and interaction is only verbal.

Scheduling is far easier, particularly when the meeting involves people who would otherwise have to travel from different locations.

Issues are dealt with in a more timely manner.

While telephone conferencing is increasing in usage, there are some disadvantages that should be recognized:

Meeting can be more difficult to lead or direct without nonverbal clues.

It is more difficult to know when one can contribute to the conversation because the speaker cannot be seen.

Discussions of complex or highly sensitive issues may not be appropriate because of the lack of visual interaction and nonverbal clues.

Teleconferencing meetings that involve a number of people and topics for discussion need an agenda, background documents, and the like, the same as for any other meeting. These topics are addressed in Chapter 2.

Whatever the format or context for meetings, though, there will be limitations on the appropriateness, which must be acknowledged along with the benefits.

Limitations of Meetings

Meetings are not a panacea—an improvement in meetings will not ensure that all decisions are made in a timely fashion and that the right decisions are always made, nor will more effective meetings necessarily result in greater consensus among all individuals affected by specific decisions. Well-run meetings do not result in quality decisions; these must rely on the clear, objective, and imaginative thinking of individuals. A well-run meeting will not result in acceptance of what is truly a bad decision, since it should still be recognized as a bad decision. A well-run meeting without follow-up will not result in acceptance and understanding of management decisions. It is important to establish reasonable expectations regarding what purpose meetings serve and the contributions that can be made through this process, and then to have members of the library develop skills and abilities to make meetings the effective tool that they can be.

When Not to Have a Meeting

Meetings do not waste time; people waste time. Time is wasted in meetings when professionals do not know how to best use them to accomplish a specific goal, including recognizing when a meeting is not the best way to accomplish a particular task or solve a specific problem.

An important way to minimize the drain that meetings have on an organization is to reduce the number of meetings that are held. This reduction is often more difficult than it appears, because while individuals complain about meetings they are seldom willing to give up *their* meetings. They may feel that they will lose out on participating in important decisions or, more disturbing, not be considered very important themselves if they are not involved in meetings. Even when individuals have done little to improve the quality of meetings in which they participate, they are often still reluctant to suggest fewer meetings or none at all.

In addition to learning the necessary skills to conduct and participate in quality meetings, staff also require criteria to measure the absolute necessity of a meeting to achieve the desired results.

When is it best not to hold a meeting? Some questions can help determine whether a meeting is really required and will be productive:

Are you able to describe the result that you want from this meeting?

Can the desired result be achieved more effectively with phone calls, via electronic mail, or a memorandum?

Is there a need for discussion, or has a decision already been made? Even if a decision has been made, is it a sensitive issue requiring explanation and an opportunity for people to discuss it further before it is implemented?

If you are calling the meeting, are you prepared, and have you provided the necessary background information to prepare other participants?

Have you considered who the key people are for the meeting? Will they be able to attend?

Have you considered the cost of the meeting's time as represented by the salaries of the people to attend? Is the cost worth the result that you have identified?

There are, of course, reasons for meetings that are not measurable in concrete terms. You may be trying to create a sense of cohesiveness within a group or to build morale, or as an administrator you may need to respond to the need for staff to hear from you personally. Then the results may be more abstract but nonetheless valid. However, most meetings do not fall into this category, and the above checklist can be used to ensure that meetings are held only when they are the most efficient and effective way to get work accomplished.

Conclusion

Meetings in all their forms and formats, purposes, and structure will continue to offer a way in which to address the many pressures on libraries—declining financial support, increased expectation for quality services and productivity, dramatic changes in the information environment, and a cultural environment in which professionals, indeed most staff, will expect greater opportunities for contributing to the decision-making process.

Tobia and Becker see meetings as a fundamental way in which organizations will respond to these pressures:

A new urgency is connected with meetings. As participation becomes key to winning the competitive wars of the 1990s, companies have a greater need to improve the effectiveness of meetings. . . . Managers are asking many technical people and workers at lower levels to participate in problem solving, decision-making, and planning meetings, but these employees have little experience working in group settings.[29]

Meetings will continue to take many forms in libraries, from those that are strictly informational, to departmental meetings that resolve operational problems, to those that involve complex and costly operations decision-making. In all of these settings, there should be a commitment to improving the quality of each and every meeting. Clearly, meetings that will have the greatest impact on the organization require immediate and sustained attention to ensure that library professionals have a voice in determining the shape and course of future library service.

Library professionals should recognize the "competitive wars" that their organizations face, and accept responsibility for ensuring that meetings become an effective tool for organization and personal success.

Notes

1. Lee Sproull and Sara Kiesler, *Connections: New Ways of Working in the Networked Organization* (Cambridge, Mass.: MIT Press, 1992), 25.
2. Michael Schrage, *Shared Minds: The New Technologies of Collaboration* (New York: Random House, 1990), 119.
3. Norman B. Sigband, "Meeting with Success," *Personnel Journal* (May 1985), 48.
4. William L. Williams, Elaine Biech, Malcolm P. Clark, "Increased Productivity through Effective Meetings," *Technical Communication* (November 1987), 264.
5. Peter M. Tobia and Martin C. Becker, "Making the Most of Meeting Time," *Training & Development Journal* (August 1990), 34.
6. David Pearce Snyder and Gregg Edwards, "America in the 1990s: An Economy in Transition, a Society under Stress," paper presented at the American Library Association Annual Meeting, Atlanta, Ga., 1991 (Washington, D.C.: E. S. Press, 1991).
7. Rosabeth Moss Kanter, "The Change Masters" in *Innovation and Entrepreneurship in the American Corporation* (New York: Simon & Schuster, 1983), 22.
8. James B. Quinn and Christopher E. Gagnon, "Will Services Follow Manufacturing into Decline?" *Harvard Business Review* (Nov.–Dec. 1986), 95.
9. David Osborne, "Government That Means Business," *New York Times Magazine* (March 1, 1992), 24.
10. Schrage, *Shared Minds*, 6, xxiii.
11. Kanter, "The Change Masters," 28.

12. Peter F. Drucker, *Management: Tasks, Responsibilities, Practices* (New York: Harper, 1974), 559–563.
13. Ibid., 567.
14. Kanter, "The Change Masters," 28.
15. Drucker, *Management*, 567.
16. Tom Peters, *Thriving on Chaos: Handbook for a Management Revolution* (New York: Harper & Row, 1987), 356–357.
17. Drucker, *Management*, 566.
18. Katherine W. Hawkins, "Implementing Team Management in the Modern Library," *Library Administration & Management* (Winter 1990), 12.
19. Gerald R. Lowell and Maureen Sullivan, "Self-Management in Technical Services: The Yale Experience," *Library Administration & Management* (Winter 1990), 23.
20. Peters, *Thriving on Chaos*, 440.
21. Kanter, "The Change Masters," 257.
22. Schrage, *Shared Minds*, 134.
23. Sproull and Kiesler, 26.
24. Ibid., 31.
25. Schrage, *Shared Minds*, 126.
26. Donald E. Riggs, "Productivity Increases in Public Services: Are Expert Systems the Answer?" *Journal of Library Management* 9 (Summer 1988), 89.
27. Ibid., 96.
28. Ibid., 97.
29. Tobia and Becker, "Making the Most of Meeting Time," 34.

Effective Meetings: Basic Ingredients

A meeting is a "cul de sac where ideas are lured and quietly strangled."[1]

Meetings are ubiquitous in life, no matter the organization environment—social and community groups, religious, political and professional organizations, as well as the work environment— but still we struggle with the frustration of ineffective meetings and rejoice, though most often quietly, when we experience a quality meeting.

Why is the process of meeting so difficult, so loaded with problems? While there is nothing inexplicable or mysterious about the meeting process, it is fraught with difficulties because of the relationships among people, the power and influence that exists within an organization, and the more general difficulty of creating an environment in which individuals can speak openly about issues. Because meetings are a way of life in libraries and because they present a complex setting within which to accomplish the work of the organization, there is considerable need for library professionals to develop an understanding and skills to both plan and conduct as well as to contribute to effective meetings.

The focus in improving meetings should be shifted from the simplistic idea of saving time to one that focuses on learning to use meeting time in a constructive and creative way. The focus on saving time is likely to result in avoiding meetings even when they offer the best way to accomplish the work required, or in limiting meeting time artificially so that issues are not explored fully. When individuals approach meetings with a grudging acceptance of the requirement to put in an appearance, they will usually be looking for ways to reduce the infringement on their time. This attitude may translate into remaining silent in the meeting, agreeing to a proposal even though one remains unconvinced it is viable, discouraging others from contributing—all behaviors intended to end the meeting as quickly as possible rather than achieving the objective of the meeting.

A shift to improving meetings (not eliminating or avoiding them) establishes a different set of expectations and requires a different set of behaviors from everyone participating. What is required is a commitment by both meeting conveners and participants to develop understanding and skill for using meetings successfully, and a willingness to exercise discipline and responsibility in every meeting. The focus in this chapter is on the basic ingredients of meetings and the role and responsibilities of all participants in creating successful results.

Types of Meetings

In order to understand the purpose and dynamics of meetings, a first step is to recognize the different objectives that meetings serve within the organization. While all meetings have a primary goal, often multiple goals exist within the context of any one meeting. The following categories for describing the purpose or goals of a meeting are helpful only in that they may assist with planning for a meeting by answering the first and most fundamental question—why should this meeting be held?

Information and Briefing Meetings

The primary objective of the information or briefing meeting is to provide the appropriate people with an update on projects or situations, or to alert them to events that are anticipated or planned.

The meeting is most often called by administrators or managers, and, too often, the communication pattern in such meetings is for the person calling the meeting to do all of the talking and those attending simply to listen. However, the informational meeting does provide an opportunity for attendees to ask questions about policies or announcements.

This type of meeting is the one in which most people become restless, if not resentful, and for valid reasons. They have only a passive role in the meeting; they are there to receive ideas or decisions and not to contribute or respond. Because of this role, the participants may feel that their time is being wasted and may wonder why the person calling the meeting did not simply issue the information in a memorandum.

The limitations of the information meeting should almost beg those most likely to call such a meeting (typically managers or supervisors) to be cautious in asking staff to spend their time in this way. An informational meeting is most appropriate when combined with other objectives, such as ensuring that people understand a sensitive or complicated new policy: for example, how the administration intends to respond to a budget crisis.

Individuals calling such a meeting need to understand the limitations and the likely frustration of participants. Meeting attendees also should seek ways to contribute in such settings, including listening more attentively and understanding the value of such meetings for the group beyond the concrete information provided.

Problem Identification and Solution Meetings

The problem identification and solution meeting is fairly common in libraries and ranges from handling a workflow problem in a particular unit such as acquisition or circulation to responding to a complaint regarding service.

While the process for such a meeting may appear straightforward, all too frequently individuals rush to find a solution before they fully clarify the problem. The problem identification step is often given too little attention, resulting in an inappropriate or inadequate solution that requires further attention at a later date in possibly another meeting.

The person convening this meeting will need first to clarify the problem, then to ensure that the right people are invited to the meeting, and then, at the meeting, allow sufficient time to fully explore the problem. Depending on the complexity, exploring the problem may take far more time than anticipated, and more than one meeting may be required to actually identify solutions to a problem, particularly if professionals are to avoid the trap of the "we've always done it this way" response.

During the meeting in which the group explores how to address a problem, the meeting convener should request the participants' options for a solution rather than a single "fix." In all cases, the participants should be asked to consider all aspects of the situation to ensure that the real problem will be addressed. Finally, individuals should be required to consider the implications of each option, including costs, political ramifications, impact on other library operations, and the like.

Planning Meetings

The planning meeting differs from the problem-solving meeting because the focus is on creating, not repairing, designing rather than fixing.

Planning consists of both a strategic or long-term focus as well as addressing immediate short-term needs. A planning meeting often centers around new services or products, new directions, and priorities. Short-term planning is usually focused at the departmental level and what can be achieved within a year or two, while strategic planning suggests the broader organizational context with a time frame of five or more years.

The use of an analytical planning model for such meetings will prove to be valuable in assisting the professionals in maintaining a clear focus on the issue at hand while giving them specific steps that they can move through to coordinate the necessary planning activities. Appendix A contains an example of a planning model.

Conflict Resolution Meetings

The conflict resolution meeting is distinct in that the conflict is usually not centered on policy or procedures but involves disagreements between individuals. These disagreements may be between a library staff member and a patron, between a supervisor and an employee, or between coworkers. Whatever the situation, the professional conducting this meeting likely has to mediate between individuals who are upset and may even be reluctant participants in the meeting. While it is important in such situations to focus on the issue and to move beyond the personalities of the individuals involved in the conflict, it is also critical to recognize and respond to the feelings of the individuals involved. This meeting is one of the more difficult to manage effectively because of the high level of emotion that may be present—all the more reason for the individual calling the meeting to clarify immediately the results desired from the meeting.

Training Meetings

Most often, training sessions (workshops, presentations, seminars) are not viewed as organizational meetings, although the same requirement for realizing a benefit from the investment of staff time to participate exists as with any other meeting. In fact, because of the critical nature of the training process, combining the learning by staff of how to perform activities as well as their development of confidence and commitment in the performance of responsibilities, training sessions represent one of the more demanding meeting contexts held in the library. Poorly organized and conducted training sessions may contribute to a high degree of frustration, which then is reflected in poor service and low productivity. Quality training leads to effective and efficient service and staff who recognize the value of their contribution. Successful training requires a careful analysis of knowledge and skill needs, an understanding and appreciation of the participants or audience, and a facilitator who has specialized skills for the training environment.

The same expectations for internal staff training meetings also apply to user education sessions.

Motivational Meetings

Establishing and maintaining a sense of cohesiveness, commitment, and enthusiasm among a group of library staff or among members of a library advisory board is an ongoing challenge for library managers and administrators. In order to meet this challenge, regular contact is needed so that there are ample opportunities for ideas and views to be contributed by all members of a particular department, unit, or working group. Dialogue among those directly involved with departmental activities or projects provides individuals with a sense of being a member of a team that is working together toward a particular goal or goals.

Therefore, an important element of many meetings, and occasionally the primary purpose of a meeting, is to address in some capacity this central aspect of any group—the members' relationship to one another and their feelings about their work and the larger organization. Seldom is this a stated agenda item, unless a problem has been identified related to working relationships or staff morale. Instead, meetings sometimes should be called (even though the topic might be addressed adequately through a memorandum or electronic mail) to provide an opportunity for interacting to maintain that sense of cohesiveness and commitment to the group rather than only to individual responsibilities.

In large libraries, many staff will have little contact on a regular basis with administrators. Meetings to which all staff are invited can provide a way for everyone to hear from the leadership in the organization—to hear unfiltered the perspective of those in key positions. The information often could be issued in a memorandum or the staff newsletter, but the meeting offers all staff the opportunity to hear directly from these individuals, to feel that they are part of the bigger picture no matter what their particular position in the organization.

By being alert to the variety of purposes served by a meeting, the meeting planner has a framework for structuring the meeting in terms of agenda and participants, and for establishing reasonable expectations for results.

Beyond the objectives for meetings, the professional also will want to consider the type of settings in which meetings occur, because each one requires consideration of format and approach in creating an effective meeting.

Settings for Meetings

Meetings occur between a supervisor and staff, among colleagues or peers, between library administrators and an advisory or managing board, and between library staff and users or patrons. Each of these combinations suggests not only content but, to some extent, the way in which the meeting is conducted, from establishing the agenda—both on what to include and the priority of issues to be addressed—to identifying who should attend and their viewpoints, and to determining how best to facilitate the meeting in terms of participation. There are no definitive guidelines, no cookbook approaches to ensure success, although factors about each setting should be considered in order to create a more effective meeting.

Internal Meetings

Library meetings may occur between supervisors and staff, a group of supervisors, or a group of nonsupervisory professionals. While internal meetings benefit from the individuals' knowledge regarding the issues and operations of the library as well as their knowledge of one another, this knowledge also may be a barrier in addressing problems or initiating new activities.

Meetings between managers and staff have the obvious hindrance before the meeting even begins—the difference in power among those attending. Tobia and Becker call meetings "metaphors for power relationships,"[2] and yet the issue of power is seldom acknowledged openly in libraries. Library professionals generally talk about working in a collegial environment with the implied assumption of shared responsibility and almost never acknowledge the reality that managers and supervisors retain a considerable amount of power because of their positions. When not acknowledged, power remains a potential barrier to achieving an environment in which to exchange ideas, air disagreements, reach a decision, or determine a recommendation to be made.

In addition, individuals come to a staff meeting with their relationships already established from day-to-day contact. It is not realistic to expect the meeting participants to alter their existing behaviors in the period of an hour or two during which they convene to address specific topics. In fact, staff may feel compelled to reinforce the positions and relationships that exist outside the meeting, and real battles may emerge as individuals struggle not over the substance of an issue but over position and perceived power.

Power differential and existing relationships can be overcome in the meeting context but only by addressing these same issues within the day-to-day organizational environment. Meetings cannot be successful as a planning, problem-solving, or staff development vehicle in the library organization unless they are a natural outgrowth of an operational environment in which respect and responsibility exist among all staff, and in which healthy disagreement is cultivated without punishment for divergent opinions or viewpoints. In other words, productive internal meetings result from a productive work environment. The person facilitating the internal meeting can use several techniques to minimize factors that may have an adverse impact on staff meetings:

- Articulate outside of the meeting environment the expectation that staff are to work collaboratively with one another, to view themselves not as individuals defending their turf but as members of a team.
- Establish a reward system that recognizes accomplishments of group efforts, not only individual efforts.
- Begin each meeting with a statement that participants will share responsibility for the quality of the meeting and that a variety of opinions are needed and disagreements are acceptable as long as they focus on issues, not personalities.
- Rotate the responsibility for chairing or facilitating a regular staff meeting, since individuals are more likely to be supportive of colleagues knowing they will want this same support when they assume this role.

Even in internal meetings in which participants are peers and no supervisors are present, the issue of perceived power differences among participants and the effect of existing relationships may create serious limitations unless individuals seek to overcome these barriers. A fundamental shift needs to occur within library organizations from a hierarchical structure (whether based on a supervisory hierarchy, hierarchy of years of experience, or professional versus support staff) to one that is built on a network construct.

In a network organization, individuals work together to solve problems regardless of departments, divisions, position, or status. The network organization model stresses the use of people's talent and expertise to address problems and to achieve innovative approaches to service. Further, communication, cooperation, and collaboration occur within the network organization as commitment to the entire organization and its objectives replaces singular loyalty to a department or unit. A shift in the library organization structure and culture could have a profound impact on the quality of internal meetings, since they are a reflection of the communication and work pattern in the library and not a distinct and isolated process.

External Meetings

Meetings involving individuals outside of the library organization suggest other types of issues that require attention in determining a structure and process for the meeting. Power is no less an issue in this environment, though who holds the most powerful role or even the relationships among the meeting participants may be less clear. For instance, a meeting between the library director and an advisory board may be affected by whether the board is strictly advisory or retains the right to renew or continue the director's contract.

The exercise of power in the external situation is usually subtle. On one hand, the library director or other professional conducting an external meeting does not want to play a passive role, confusing service with being a servant. There should be a willingness to assume the authority and confidence of a professional while also being open to suggestions and criticisms from those outside of the library organization.

On the other hand, librarians have to be careful when meeting with library patrons to avoid assuming the posture of ownership of the library and the superiority of their knowledge. This posture is intimidating and may well limit the willingness of library users to ask questions or pursue specific issues in any depth for fear that they will be made to look foolish, or worse, receive poor service in the future. Users also may become angry in the face of arrogant, possessive, or stubborn behavior on the part of librarians, and this anger may eventually affect important constituency support for the library.

Other factors must be considered when planning external meetings with individuals who are not themselves part of the library organization.

Preparation. The professionals conducting or acting as representatives to a meeting of the library advisory board or a similar library-affiliated group will more than likely have to be responsible for advance preparation for all meeting details, from the agenda to the room arrangements. The background materials provided to the participants may have to be more encompassing in background and scope while also not burying people in too much detail.

"Libraryese." It is critical to be cautious about the use of jargon or reference to programs or procedures without explanation in external meetings. If the library representatives are not careful about this, participation will be severely limited, and participants might possibly be offended because they feel patronized or excluded from the discussion.

Time limitations. Individuals outside the library may not be interested or able to spend as much time exploring issues in all of their permutations as library staff would, and therefore they will appreciate having information synthesized for them. In addition, they also will expect that meetings will begin and end on time.

Introductions. External meetings require that introductions be made so that participants are comfortable with one another and therefore able to focus on the agenda rather than wondering who is sitting next to him or her.

The success of both internal and external meetings rests not only in sound organization prior to and at the meeting but also in understanding the dynamics of the individuals that will be brought together. Indeed, the planning for a meeting should include consideration of the views, perspective, and requirements of the participants in order to anticipate how to conduct an effective meeting.

One measure of a successful meeting is that "all participants, not just the leader, get something out of it."[3] In order to achieve this involvement by all participants, the meeting planner should give attention to the setting—the context of every meeting, including the participants and the nature of their relationship to one another—and should also address the other requirements for creating an effective meeting.

Planning for Meetings

The effort put into planning for every meeting—no matter how routine and standard in the library—has consequences for the quality of the meeting. Each individual organizing a meeting should move through a planning process in order to generate more productive results from this means of organization communication and work.

Meeting Objectives

The very first step in the planning process is for the professional who is about to call a meeting to ask, why have this meeting? what do I want to accomplish? Tobia and Becker state that the person should also ask, "when the meeting is over, how will I know that it was a success?"[4]

These questions should be asked before every meeting, even those that are routinely scheduled, and the meeting planner should write down the response as a mechanism for focusing and clarifying the purpose of a meeting. If this preliminary procedure appears to be too much effort in planning for a meeting, take a few moments to estimate the cost to the library: multiply the average salary rate of the meeting participants by the anticipated length of the meeting. For example, an average meeting in a library might be one and a half hours, with five professionals in attendance at an average annual salary of $35,000, plus an additional 29 percent of their salaries in benefits. This will make the average hourly salary and benefit cost for each professional $24.80. To the meeting time, add the preparation time for each professional of an hour or more, the time they need to actually get to the meeting from their offices or work areas, and start-up time they will require when returning to their primary responsibilities after the meeting. With a total of three and a half hours required for each professional to participate in this one meeting, the approximate meeting cost to the library is over $400. While not a large sum, surely this amount is large enough to suggest that the meeting planner should have a clear objective for holding a meeting before staff resources—the most expensive item in the library's budget—are wasted!

Because meetings are expensive in people's time as well as a potential source of frustration and demoralization, the meeting planner has a considerable responsibility to identify the objectives for a meeting. Some examples of meeting objectives or results follow:

Review the backlog in shelving to identify where problems exist and to identify solutions in order to achieve a specified daily goal.

Discuss the options for responding to mandated budget reductions in order to prepare a proposal for central administration within a week that will describe recommended service and operations reductions and the impact of each reduction on clientele.

Review with department clerical employees assignments, schedules, and problems that have arisen in the past month, in order to ensure each employee is appropriately trained and understands performance expectations in all regards; to obtain feedback from the staff on any difficulties they might be experiencing.

Discuss with the binding company representative a more frequent pickup and delivery of materials.

When the meeting planner is unable to state an objective for a meeting or to describe specific results to be accomplished, then it is likely that the meeting should not be held.

The Agenda

Once the objectives for a meeting are clearly stated, establishing an agenda is the next step. Developing an agenda is the most obvious requirement for an effective meeting; nonetheless, it is amazing how frequently this basic ingredient to a well-run and focused meeting is overlooked. When there is an agenda it consists too often of only a few words that indicate little to the participants in terms of what they will be expected to accomplish at the meeting. Using the objectives as a guide and considering the length of time in which the meeting is to be conducted (one hour, half a day, and so forth), the meeting planner should identify the specific topics to be covered during the meeting. Depending on the type of meeting, more than one person may be involved in establishing an agenda, or a general call may go out to meeting participants to suggest agenda items. However the agenda is developed (by one person or a group process), the following factors are required:

A decision as to the exact topics or issues to be included on the agenda

Priority order for the topics to be sure that the most critical issues are, indeed, covered in the time available

An estimate of time required for each topic so that the meeting chair or facilitator can guide the discussion and individual presentations within this time structure

Identification of individuals responsible for each particular topic and the role that the person will play at the meeting.

The actual format of an agenda can also help focus the discussion by the participants during the meeting. If the agenda remains a mystery to those who will attend because it contains too little information, the participants will arrive at the meeting unprepared and possibly resentful because they may be put on the spot to discuss or react to an issue for which they are unprepared. An agenda should be developed that provides participants with more information about the topic and about the topic's discussion. The following format provides an example of how to create an agenda that is a useful document to the meeting chair and the attendees.

Agenda for Management Meeting

Discussion topics:

1. Review and discuss status of budget situation after two budget quarters in relation to budget needs in general services and personnel.
   Action expected: Arrive at decision regarding major expenditure commitments for next budget quarter. (45 minutes)

2. Discussion of proposal for establishing a fee for nonprimary clientele (document previously distributed).
   Action expected: Determine whether to support this proposal with any modifications that are agreed to at the meeting. (30 minutes)

This sample format provides an expanded statement on the topic, but most importantly it indicates the *action expected* from those attending the meeting. This format alerts individuals in advance to their responsibility at the meeting, and it should encourage everyone to be prepared when they arrive at the meeting, having not only reviewed any materials distributed but having already thought about the issue.

Several other aspects to developing an agenda need to be addressed for each and every meeting: the advance distribution of the agenda, the value of a timed agenda, and identification of individuals who will play a key role in presenting agenda items.

In order for the agenda to be helpful, it should be distributed sufficiently in advance of the meeting so that everyone will have time to prepare. Typically the agenda will be distributed a week to three weeks before the meeting depending on the scope and complexity of the meeting content. While most people may prepare for a meeting fairly close to the actual schedule, nonetheless, they resent being presented with a full and complicated agenda with a large amount of reading materials a day or two prior to the meeting. Distributing the agenda too close to the meeting also makes the meeting planner appear to be disorganized and out of control— not a good way to begin a meeting, and it is more likely to result in participants who are unprepared. The meeting planner needs to set the tone for organization and preparation, meaning an agenda that is clear in topics to be discussed and action to be taken, and distributed sufficiently in advance of the meeting.

In addition to stating the topics clearly and the action required for each, all agendas should have time specified for each topic. By establishing a time estimate for each topic, the agenda provides a framework within which the meeting facilitator as well as participants can focus their comments on the most germane issues of a topic. A timed agenda encourages participants to keep their comments focused on the subject if they know the "clock is ticking." A timed agenda also allows all meeting participants to assist with the meeting process and pace by staying within the specified time allotted. In addition, with a timed agenda, meeting participants arrive at a meeting with an understanding that the meeting will be conducted with seriousness and a respect for everyone's time.

Despite the benefits of a timed agenda, many individuals who provide agenda items will respond to a request for a time estimate with all manner of avoidance, such as not knowing the number or type of questions the participants will have, not being able or willing to estimate the time they will need to present background information, and so forth. The meeting planner should reject any such excuses and require that all agenda items have time estimates attached.

Finally, as the agenda is being developed, the meeting planner should identify individuals who will be responsible for making presentations and possibly directing discussion around a particular topic. When appropriate, individual assignments should be noted directly on the agenda. A meeting participant should not be taken by surprise upon arriving at a meeting to find that he or she is expected to provide the background, to defend a particular policy proposal, or to facilitate the discussion among those attending.

While a well-constructed agenda cannot singly ensure a quality meeting, it will be almost impossible to have such a meeting without this document. With an agenda that is clear and specific, individuals will understand their responsibilities for preparation as well as what is expected of them at the meeting itself.

Selecting Meeting Participants

If the meeting that is being planned is not a staff meeting where attendance is defined by assignments within a department, then careful thought should be given to whom to include in a meeting or to appoint to a committee or task force. White states that "the question of what each individual uniquely and specifically brings to the process must be addressed in making committee appointments because committees are expensive."[5]

For example, a committee is being established to advise the library administration on the personnel program (policies, procedures, and specific activities), or a task force is being set up to determine the inclusion of nonbibliographic data into the online catalog. Who should participate? What is the knowledge and skill that will be needed? Goleman points out that a group can work well "when there is a balance between a sense of solidarity and a focus on the task at hand and when the task is appropriate to the group."[6] Goleman also indicates that success occurs when group members "have a high degree of diversity of both experiences and points of view . . . [and] that most people . . . had the same levels of persuasiveness, expressiveness and assertiveness."[7]

These criteria may be difficult to apply rigorously in the library in all cases. Nonetheless, it is helpful to consider such criteria in identifying who should participate in a specific meeting or an ongoing assignment for a committee. It is also a way for the planner to assess the strengths and weaknesses of a group that will be meeting together to make a recommendation on a major operational policy decision or to develop an implementation plan for a new system.

In addition to identifying who should attend a meeting, there is the equally important task of recognizing who should *not* attend a particular meeting or sit on a specific committee. Aside from the obvious problem of wasting the time of individuals who have no contribution to make at a particular meeting, the wrong individuals may be disruptive to the work of the group. Focusing on who is absolutely essential to a meeting or the work of a committee helps prevent overly large groups. Large groups create potential barriers to achieving a quality meeting, including too many people trying to talk, a number of people who not only do not contribute but are distracting through their silence as well as their body language, and general confusion over the purpose of a meeting when people are included who do not have a clear contribution to make.

Preparation

After developing an agenda and identifying meeting participants, the meeting planner must determine the materials to be used during the meeting and those to be distributed in advance; the arrangements for the meeting room including location, size, physical arrangement of seating, and the equipment required; and what record of the meeting is necessary and who will act as recorder.

When the agenda is distributed, materials that are required reading for the meeting should be included. If there is something specific the participants are expected to do in advance of a meeting, it should be stated clearly in the agenda. Specifically, indicate if they should read the distributed materials and be prepared to respond on the content and in what way; or if they should be prepared to take a position on a particular proposal or offer alternatives; or if participants who are supervisors should discuss a particular topic with staff and be prepared to represent not only their opinions but those of their staff at the meeting. Whatever is expected should be clearly stated as part of the agenda document or cover memo with the appropriate materials distributed at the same time.

The meeting planner also needs to consider what appropriate visuals might be used during the meeting to improve the organization of ideas and information, thereby keeping the meeting focused. By making visuals more interesting and stimulating, the meeting planner can in this way encourage attention to the issue under discussion and contribute to greater retention of the information presented. In order to accomplish their purpose, visual aids should contribute in the following way:

- Clarify and reinforce the presenter's message.
- Highlight key information.
- Focus the participant's attention on one concept or idea at a time.
- Appear simple and uncluttered.
- Be easy to interpret.
- Be easy to view—legible, attractive, pleasing.[8]

The meeting planner will have to consider if a specific topic or issue lends itself to visual materials. Too often, planners consider visual materials to be no more than a projection of charts and numbers that are rather dull to view and, at times, impossible to see from every location in a meeting room. Readily available options exist for creating visual aids, from slides and video to computer software for generating graphic displays of data and text, as well as the standard overhead transparencies and flip charts. In addition to providing background information for the participants, flip charts or overhead transparencies also may provide a useful way to record key points in a discussion, assisting the meeting convener to keep people focused on an issue and moving forward while generating a record of the decisions reached in a meeting. Depending on the sophistication of the visual materials desired, the planner will need to allow sufficient time to develop quality materials.

Equipment needs for a meeting are related to the determination of what visual aids will be employed. Whatever equipment is needed, it must be available in the room well in advance of the meeting and checked thoroughly to be sure that it is operational with requisite spare parts. The person who will be using the equipment must indeed know how to do so, including handling mishaps.

Delaying a meeting to wait for the late delivery of equipment, to replace a burned out bulb on a projector, or to handle other aspects of equipment setup is disruptive. The confusion that results when delays occur will distract participants from their primary purpose and may color their view of the entire meeting and the issues to be discussed.

Next, the physical arrangements for a meeting, particularly one involving a large number of people or lasting several hours, should be addressed. An unpleasant or uncomfortable room will have a negative effect on participants and the quality of the meeting. The space for a meeting should be adequate for the size of the group. Individuals should be able to sit comfortably with their materials at hand and to take notes without being squashed against one another. The arrangement of tables and chairs should allow for and encourage a free flow of conversation and interaction among the participants.

Again, the objective of the meeting is what should guide a room arrangement, though the size of a group may limit options. For a meeting where the agenda focuses on problem-solving or planning, a high degree of interaction among participants is desirable. Meeting attendees will need to see one another in order to facilitate dialogue. They need not only to hear one another but to gauge reactions and to establish interactions by seeing one another's body language. The arrangement of the furniture for a discussion-focused meeting also should not reinforce a perception of a hierarchy or favored status among participants—there is a reason why international peace or summit conferences use a round table whenever possible and spend considerable time in determining who will sit where. When holding a large meeting in which the primary purpose is for someone to provide information and respond to questions, a theatre or classroom format is acceptable. Specific information regarding seating arrangements can be found in Appendix A.

The location of the equipment should be considered in conjunction with the room arrangement since the use of flip charts, overhead transparencies, slide projectors, a video monitor, and the like will affect the placement of the participants. Obviously everyone has to have a sightline to the materials being used, to be able to clearly see the visuals no matter where they are located in the room.

The final aspect of preparation that the meeting planner needs to address is what type of record of the meeting is required and appropriate. If a record is necessary, then the information wanted should be determined in advance, such as a summary of key points or a verbatim record, attributing or not attributing comments to individuals, and an indication of actions resulting or to be initiated from the meeting. The planner also should determine how the meeting content will be recorded (will a meeting participant be asked to act as recorder, for example, or will a secretary attending the meeting be asked to record minutes) and expectation for distribution of the minutes (are they only for the participants, or will they be broadly distributed).

All of these points need to be determined in advance based on the content, complexity, and sensitivity of the issues to be discussed as well any requirements of the library and its parent institution for making such information publicly available. An efficient way to provide a record of what a group has discussed and acted upon (or even postponed) is to create a record of actions taken for each agenda topic and the follow-up required and by whom. If appropriate, a brief summary of the rationale for a particular action also could be part of the official record so that staff and others understand why something was decided, not only what was decided.

The success of meetings begins with the advance preparation for all aspects of the meeting itself from the agenda through the arrangement of the room itself. Overlooking any aspect of this process will result in the potential for a poor meeting. The time invested in advance planning will be well worthwhile when the participants come together because they will benefit from a well-organized, focused meeting.

Conducting a Meeting

While preparation by a meeting planner is essential, even the most thorough planning in constructing an agenda, identifying participants, and making the room arrangements will not result in an effective meeting without addressing the human dimension aspect of a meeting. The planning provides the foundation on which the meeting convener must now construct an effective outcome through people who participate in the meeting. The success of every meeting rests with the individuals who have been brought together to solve a problem, design a new program or service, or consider the impact of a new policy. Dutton suggests a way to consider this aspect of the meeting by focusing on process, content, and feelings, which he considers to be the "fundamental building blocks" of a meeting. He defines these as:

> *Content*—people's opinions, expertise, information, suggestions, data, and the like.
>
> *Process*—setting priorities, identifying pros and cons of an issue/problem, soliciting opinions, suggesting timelines, exploring, defining, focusing.
>
> *Feelings*—a gauge of the meeting reflected in confusion, frustration, boredom, anxiety or dissatisfaction of participants as compared to involvement, commitment, enthusiasm.[9]

The relative importance of each of these human dimensions will differ depending on the type of meeting and the relationship of participants. Nonetheless, the meeting convener requires considerable leadership skill and advanced planning to achieve a balance among these three dimensions so that the results wanted from the meeting occur.

Role of Meeting Convener

The person who conducts a meeting, the convener, has a significant contribution to make in achieving the results desired from the activity. Success in this role often is a major challenge depending on the participants, the volatility of the topics to be discussed, and other factors that may come into play. Kiechel indicates that leadership is tested in meetings with the "competing factions jockeying for advantage, blowhards wanting to drone on interminably, and the critical information often withheld by the stony and silent."[10] He concludes that meetings are the place where true leadership ability surfaces. The convener will need to focus on process, content, and the feelings of individuals present while also being cognizant of the power relationships among the participants and the hidden agendas that may be operating. The convener should be adept at consensus building and conflict management while also exercising direction without being controlling.

In advance of a meeting, the external convener should consider how he or she might address meeting process, content, and participants' feelings in relation to the topics to be discussed and the personality, knowledge, and style of the individuals who will be participating.

Process

A focus on the process of the meeting should include the following actions:

> *Begin and end the meeting on time.* Meeting participants will appreciate the fact that you respect their time and the many demands on their schedule and energy, and they, in turn, are likely to focus their attention to achieving the objectives of the meeting.

> *Establish orientation and context for every meeting.* The meeting facilitator should provide comments at the beginning of a meeting to review the goals of the meeting and the format to be followed, background on the issues or topics to be discussed, and the range of possible actions that the group might take or is expected to take. With this context the meeting facilitator can reiterate the expectation that all attendees will contribute to the discussion and the recommendations or decisions to be reached.

> *Summarize frequently.* Frequent summaries by the meeting facilitator assist in keeping the group focused both in terms of the agenda and the schedule while also providing an opportunity to highlight consensus reached or progress made on a particular topic. Consensus building among meeting participants is most important—and even more so in discussion of complex or contentious issues—as it aids participants in focusing on what they are able to agree on rather than feeling discouraged by those issues over which they have yet to achieve consensus.

> *Maintain meeting schedule or ask for a resetting of priorities.* If the discussion is productive but time is getting short, ask the participants how they wish to proceed—do they wish to drop other topics from the agenda or to postpone the current discussion for a later meeting, for example. Whenever possible ask the participants to take responsibility for the quality of the meeting and the direction of the discussion.

Maintaining control. While the convener does not want to dominate, he or she still needs to guide the meeting so that the group stays on target in its discussion. The convener must continually reinforce the objective of the meeting and the main points of the topic by ignoring irrelevant or tangential comments, asking the more outspoken individuals to allow others to speak, and, as needed, asking the group to indicate if they feel the discussion is appropriately focused on the topic.

Concluding the meeting. At the end of every meeting, the facilitator should provide a summary of what has been agreed to and what next steps will be taken and by whom. This summary is particularly important in a lengthy meeting when the participants could go away uncertain as to what actually has been decided and feeling that their time has been wasted. An effective convener will assist in directing the participants to a conclusion without either rushing them to a hasty, ill-considered solution before they have amply explored the problem or allowing them to avoid or postpone a decision when one is required.

Content

The content of the meeting rests with the information required to address a particular problem, issue, or new programmatic effort. Therefore the meeting convener should consider the following in determining meeting content:

Draw on expertise and diverse opinions. The reason for using a meeting to address problems or plan for new programs is to draw on the diverse expertise, experience, and views that exist within the library on particular topics. The meeting facilitator has the responsibility for using techniques and approaches to solicit a high degree of participation by everyone at the meeting. Several techniques, which are explained in detail in Appendix B, include brainstorming, the delphi method, small group process within larger groups, and the nominal group technique.

Use a problem-solving model. A group that is meeting to address an existing problem or the development and implementation of a new service will benefit from a structure within which to explore the many facets of the situation. It is not uncommon for individuals to get ahead of themselves and rather than focusing on the "what" of the topic—what is wrong, what do we want to do—instead move immediately to "how"—how do we fix the problem, avoid the situation, or implement the program. Individuals who demonstrate a capacity for "trouble shooting" or "fire-fighting" are often seen as decisive and action-oriented and are thus respected and rewarded within the library organization. While library professionals cannot afford to talk a subject to death, there does need to be a balance between rushing to find a solution and ensuring that we know first what the problem is that we want to solve. Meeting participants need to think and discuss the issues first by framing the discussion in questions, not in answers, so that adequate information along with diverse views and opinions surface.

The meeting convener could provide a problem-solving model that the meeting attendees could then follow so that they examine every aspect of a situation before moving to resolution. Appendix B contains problem-solving models that can be used or modified for different meeting situations.

Remember that disagreement is healthy. It is difficult but necessary for library professionals to learn that when disagreement over the substance of an issue exists it is valid and valuable to have it expressed openly. Too often, library professionals view disagreement as discourteous or rude and are uncomfortable when divergent views or even challenges are expressed in a meeting. When disagreement over a proposal or a recommendation is buried, however, tensions mount and morale declines. When professionals fail to share their views in a meeting and instead express their disagreement after a decision has been reached, disruption and dissension is more likely to occur. The frank sharing of opinions, even those in disagreement with others, is an indication of a healthy organization—one that values different talents, experiences, and viewpoints.

At the same time, when library administrators act as meeting conveners, they must be receptive to hearing the differing viewpoints and avoid responding in a negative way, particularly to those who take issue with their ideas or recommendations.

More generally, it is up to the meeting convener to encourage an open approach to exploring topics while also moving the group to a decision.

The final component that should be addressed by the meeting planner and facilitator is the feelings of the individuals participating in a meeting.

Feelings

In order to gain desired results from meetings, the facilitator should be alert to the feelings of individuals who will be participating in a meeting. The facilitator must give some thought, in advance of the meeting, to the participants and how they are likely to respond to a particular issue or topic. By being prepared in this way, the facilitator more likely will be able to frame issues and questions constructively and lead the discussion in such a way as to minimize the negative or hostile reactions by particular individuals. The first precept for any meeting facilitator, and participant for that matter, is to recognize that all behavior is communication. By acknowledging the importance of both verbal and nonverbal communication to the substance of a discussion, the meeting facilitator will be in a far better position to create an effective meeting.

Specifically, the facilitator should be alert to the nonverbal behavior of meeting participants. Disagreement, frustration, and anger are often expressed not through spoken words but through nonverbal clues that show how individuals are really responding. The meeting facilitator can either ask for a verbal expression of these nonverbal messages—which may be perceived as challenging or confrontational—or avoid direct recognition and instead build greater consensus among the other participants for a particular idea or recommendation. If the facilitator is not alert to the effect of nonverbal communication within a group, the meeting participants may not tackle the more critical issues or factions may emerge within the group.

The individual who facilitates and directs a meeting needs to be alert to these three components of meetings—process, content, and the feelings of the participants, to be cognizant of the power relationships among the participants, and to be alert to whether a hidden agenda may be operating. The meeting convener should be adept at consensus building and conflict management, and should have the skill to move the group along without dominating the discussion.

In summary, the meeting convener should exercise leadership in the following important ways, as identified in the materials issued by the 3M Corporation: "One is to guide the participants through the meeting in a logical, orderly pattern ending with the accomplishment of the meeting's purpose. The second is to encourage, and get, participation when [needed]. . . . The third is to maintain control of the meeting . . . to keep it on track and on time." The guidelines go on to offer the following cautions: encourage, don't resent, questions; be a facilitator and not a monopolizer of discussion; use humor as appropriate but don't be a constant comic; don't put anyone down in public; and, coming unprepared is worse than not coming.[11]

While the meeting convener has a critical role in certain settings, it is appropriate to select an option to the traditional approach for who conducts a meeting by using one of the following: (1) identify a neutral party to act as the facilitator, or (2) allow the group to decide to operate without an official chairperson or facilitator.

Neutral Facilitator

The selection of a neutral facilitator might be particularly useful when the topic or issues to be discussed at a meeting are of a highly sensitive or controversial nature. A facilitator, unlike a manager or project director, should not have a stake in the issues that are to be discussed. Neutral facilitators may advise on agendas and materials for the meeting, but they do not determine the content and objectives for a meeting. They develop strategies and techniques for the meeting process that will most likely result in the stated objective. While a neutral facilitator may be someone from within the library organization, most often a consultant is employed in this capacity. The neutral facilitator's role during the meeting should be to

Avoid sharing personal opinions or ideas and making evaluative comments

Challenge participants to support their views and opinions and to consider alternatives

Encourage everyone to contribute

Encourage the group to evaluate its progress.

The neutral facilitator also can be helpful in providing an evaluation after the meeting on the process, content, and the next steps.

Group Facilitating

In some settings, a specific meeting coordinator may not be necessary. Dutton has indicated that as organizations move "toward shared leadership and autonomous work groups," always looking to a single person to conduct a meeting as a way to achieve meeting effectiveness may be a mistake.[12] A meeting structure in which no one is actually in charge is most likely to be effective in small groups of five to seven and ones in which the participants already have established a constructive working relationship. The concept of shared responsibility for the outcome of all library meetings is crucial, though, no matter the size of a meeting or who is actually conducting the meeting.

While group facilitating might be an alternative to the more traditional meeting chairperson or convener, most library meetings will likely continue to operate in the more traditional fashion. The person who conducts a meeting faces a major challenge, and more of one when difficult issues must be addressed or individuals who are likely to be uncooperative attend. The role of the meeting convener requires preparation and knowledge of the issues to be discussed. Equally important, though, is for the convener to understand group dynamics, to recognize the implicit as well as explicit messages that are being sent, and to understand the culture of the organization within which the meeting is taking place.

Role of Meeting Participants

Professionals who participate in library meetings need to recognize the extent to which their contributions affect the quality of each and every meeting they attend. Tobia and Becker have pointed out that "many meeting attendants subscribe to the notion that the person who leads a meeting shoulders the responsibility for the outcome." But Tobia and Becker challenge this view when they state that "meetings are the ultimate team sport" with the burden of success falling on both the meeting planner or convener and the participants.[13] Dutton indicates that when meeting participants leave the quality of a meeting up to the chairperson, this behavior is in direct opposition to "most people's expressed goals of self-management." He suggests that an approach to improving meeting effectiveness is a model that "gives accountability to all meeting participants."[14]

It is not unusual to overhear individuals muttering as they leave a library meeting that they did not agree with the recommendation or decision that was reached, or that they felt that the meeting was a waste of time. They indeed may be the same individuals who contributed little to the discussion or who conversely dominated the discussion or interjected their own agenda into the meeting. Whatever their behavior in meetings, library professionals have a responsibility for the quality of a meeting in which they participate. If they leave a meeting feeling that it was a failure or a waste of time, then they are evaluating their own performance—and thus failure, not only the performance of the official meeting facilitator. Professionals need to recognize and to act on their responsibility and capacity for leadership in all aspects of organization life. Full participation in a meeting is one of the many opportunities that they have to affect the quality of the organization for staff and library users.

In addition, the library administration should accept responsibility for encouraging the full participation of professionals in meetings, by providing appropriate training so that individuals acquire an understanding of meeting content, structure, and process and develop the skills required for working within this environment.

Hidden Agendas

A final consideration for any meeting is the potential for a hidden agenda. The hidden agenda represents a topic or issue, attitude, or motive of an individual or several people within the group. Zaremba describes a hidden agenda as one that is a "self-serving unstated goal which drives the discussion off course."[15] Such unstated goals can be held by participants at all levels of the organization. An individual's personal agenda is not necessarily disruptive to a meeting if the personal goals merge with those that exist for the meeting.

Again the meeting planner should give some consideration to the potential for a hidden agenda prior to the meeting. Kiechel suggests that the hidden agenda might be treated similar to market or audience research so that the meeting planner asks "who are these people? what positions or interests do they represent? what will they be hoping to accomplish?" He goes on to state that the meeting planner should "give some thought to the behavior you can expect from each participant, and take prophylactic action against potential problems."[16]

During the meeting, the convener will need to determine what action to take if a participant appears to be consistently raising an issue that is not related to the topic under discussion. For instance, the convener might suggest to the person that the issue should be placed on a subsequent meeting agenda and that the person take responsibility for presenting the topic, including providing the relevant background materials and, if appropriate, several alternatives for the group to discuss in addressing the issue. Another approach is to indicate that the topic would be appropriately discussed with another set of people and not with the immediate meeting participants. In both cases, the meeting convener is offering a compromise rather than simply struggling to silence the person. In some situations, though, it will be best to ignore the inappropriate comments and for the convener to continue to encourage discussion on the issue at hand.

A more difficult situation is when several people or even the entire group appears to be operating with a hidden agenda. It will be exceedingly difficult for the facilitator to keep the meeting focused on the primary purpose in this context, and a decision will need to be made as to whether the hidden agenda should be made the primary agenda for the meeting.

The fact of a hidden agenda is a matter that should be considered prior to the meeting so that the facilitator is prepared to respond to its likelihood during the meeting. In addition, though, professionals share responsibility for eliminating hidden agendas and the disruption that results by ensuring that they do not use meetings to exercise their own agendas and goals that are unrelated to the stated objectives for the meeting.

Summary

The complexity of all personal interactions, particularly those involving a number of individuals, should never be underestimated. Meetings are here to stay in the library organization, and if they are to contribute toward organizational effectiveness and personal satisfaction, considerable effort has to be invested in both the mechanics and the relationship aspect of meetings.

The following are frequent mistakes that occur in meetings—ones to be avoided by both conveners and participants:

Ignoring the stated times to begin and end the meeting.

Setting an agenda that is unreasonable in relation to the time available.

Allowing the discussion to stray from the stated agenda topics through inattention.

Allowing individual hidden agendas to dominate.

Rushing to solutions rather than fully examining an issue.

Lack of preparation by the meeting convener and participants.

Lack of a summary at the end of the meeting on what has been agreed to and the next steps to be taken.

If everyone who attends a meeting would focus on improving these aspects of the organization of meetings, greater results could be achieved from the time invested in meetings.

In addition, though, the success of library meetings is contingent upon professionals incorporating the following values into their approach to organizational issues and working relationships:

Willingness to place the needs of the library over departmental or personal preferences or needs.

Openness to different ideas, viewpoints, and personal styles.

Willingness to listen and consider another's opinion and perspective.

An acceptance that disagreement over issues is healthy.

Generosity of spirit in working with colleagues.

Acceptance of responsibility for the quality of every meeting in which one is a participant.

If these values are combined with an improvement in the organization of meetings, library professionals are likely to see that their time spent in meetings pays dividends in the quality of decision-making and ultimately library services.

Notes

1. Alan Zaremba, "Meetings and Frustration: Practical Methods for Structuring Group Sessions," *Supervision* (August 1988), 7.
2. Peter M. Tobia and Martin C. Becker, "Making the Most of Meeting Time," *Training & Development Journal* (August 1990), 34.
3. Daniel Goleman, "Why Meetings Sometimes Don't Work," Living Arts Section, *New York Times* (March 30, 1989), 24.
4. Tobia and Becker, "Making the Most of Meeting Time," 37.
5. Herbert S. White, "White Papers: Meetings, Bloody Meetings," *Library Journal* (March 15, 1992), 61.
6. Goleman, "Why Meetings Sometimes Don't Work," 15.
7. Ibid., 24.
8. 3M Visual Systems Division, *Six Secrets to Improve Your Future Business Meetings*, 3M Austin Center, Austin, Tex., 13.
9. Darrell W. J. Dutton, "A Behavioral Approach to Meeting Effectiveness," *Training & Development Journal* (November 1987), 30–33.
10. Walter Kiechel, "How to Lead a Meeting," *Fortune* (August 29, 1988), 97.
11. 3M Visual Systems Division, *Six Secrets to Improve Your Future Business Meetings*, 17.
12. Dutton, "A Behavioral Approach to Meeting Effectiveness," 30.
13. Tobia and Becker, "Making the Most of Meeting Time," 36.
14. Dutton, "A Behavioral Approach to Meeting Effectiveness," 30.
15. Zaremba, "Meetings and Frustration," 7.
16. Kiechel, "How to Lead a Meeting," 98.

3

Effective Communication in the Meeting Environment

Merely providing an opportunity for communication does not necessarily ensure it will take place.[1]

A broad understanding of communication theory and techniques by library professionals is fundamental to successful meetings of all types and in all formats. Practicing effective interpersonal communication in addition to understanding the effects of group dynamics in the meeting environment will help ensure successful meetings. This chapter reviews concepts related to group communication and the meeting environment.

Communication Basics

Communication exists as both context and content. Context exists in at least four dimensions—physical, social, psychological, and temporal. Fisher and Ellis define communication as "a pattern of behaviors in which the acts of each communicator constrain and are constrained by the patterns created by his or her own and others' behaviors. All people who engage in communication develop an interdependent relationship with one another."[2] An understanding of the dynamics of interdependence will help meeting conveners and participants develop successful strategies for achieving results.

Content and Relationship

Two fundamental aspects of communication should be acknowledged:

- We cannot not communicate.
- All behavior is communication, and all behavior has a message value.

Communication implies a relationship between two or more people and is built on both verbal and nonverbal methods of delivering and receiving a message. The content of the message refers to some aspect of the external world both speaker and listener understand. Communication of content occurs within the existing relationship between speaker and listener.

Verbal communication may be transmitted in person, by writing, by phone, or through electronic mail. Verbal communication is discrete, consisting of words and sentences; it has a distinct beginning and end. Nonverbal communication is a powerful medium for transmitting all kinds of intended and unintended messages contained in facial expression, posture, personal space, body actions, environment, and clothing or dress. People's opinions are initially formed, whether consciously or unconsciously, from the nonverbal medium. Moreover, nonverbal communication is continuous and does not have a discrete ending like words and sentences. Researchers have identified the following dimensions of nonverbal communication:

- Kinesics: the use of one's body, facial expressions
- Poxemics: the way interpersonal space is used
- Paralanguage: how things are said: pitch, rate, loudness, inflection of speech
- Chronemics: timing of verbal exchanges.[3]

People use all of these elements to send and interpret messages. Nonverbal communication usually speaks louder than actual words. Consider what the tone of a sentence can do to its meaning if said in a positive manner or sarcastically. Body language speaks loudly at meetings, for example, when a participant exhibits disgust by sighing or shrugging rather than verbally articulating his or her concerns. These signs sometimes serve as guideposts for participants to understand each other's attitudes or reactions, which may not be as clear with other methods of communication.

Characteristics of Effective Interpersonal Communication

Meetings represent a group of people attempting to work together by establishing relationships that build on their ability to communicate. Interpersonal communication, like any form of behavior, can vary from being extremely effective to ineffective. The following characteristics of effective interpersonal communication are important in the meeting environment:

Openness. A willingnesss to reveal information about one's views and opinions relevant to the topic and a willingness to react honestly to others' comments and ideas. Recognition that disagreement is not unusual within a group of people and that allowing differences to surface is productive as groups work toward conclusions.

Empathy. An understanding of what other individuals are feeling and their perspective on issues and concerns; an attempt to understand rather than move quickly to judge.

Supportiveness. Building a nonthreatening environment where others' comments are not attacked but critically analyzed.

Positiveness. Holding a positive regard toward oneself and others, and creating a positive atmosphere that allows for productive encounters instead of negative and destructive ones.

Equality. Honoring every participant as a valuable and worthwhile human being with something to contribute. Equality of respect is what is required no matter what the participants' status within the organization or the meeting setting.

Ensuring that the characteristics of openness, empathy, supportiveness, positiveness, and equality are encouraged in meetings will help participants interact in a more positive and productive way. Individuals whose actions mirror these characteristics are focused outwardly to others. A working group exhibiting these characteristics collectively will be more effective because of the additional cohesiveness and trust they bring to the process of problem-solving and decision-making.

Interpersonal Awareness

The concept of self-awareness, basic to an understanding of inter-personal, is key to meeting success. Three dimensions of personal awareness affect interpersonel relationships, in particular the concept of self-awareness:

1. The open self represents all the information, behaviors, attitudes, feelings, desires, motivations, and ideas that are known to one's self and shared with others.
2. The blind self represents all of those things about an individual that others can see but the individual has not recognized, including such things as defensive reactions, domination of conversations, an inability or unwillingness to contribute to discussions.
3. The hidden self represents everything about oneself which is kept to oneself.

All of these "selves" interact to shape the nature of interpersonal communication, including the conduct of individuals in meetings.

Dimensions of Credibility

Credibility is another aspect of personal interactions that has an impact on the success of meetings. Establishing and maintaining credibility need to be recognized as essential in the organizational context and therefore in library meetings. The following are dimensions of credibility; each contributes to a person's credibility:

Competence: the knowledge and intelligence
ascribed to a person.

Character: the honesty or trustworthiness of a person.

Intention: the motives or intentions of a person.

Personality: the person's likability.

Dynamism: aggression, extroversion, forcefulness
of an individual.

Recognizing aspects of credibility as they apply to meeting participants allows for a more objective approach when listening to and acting upon individuals' contributions in meetings.

Feedback

The concept of feedback is crucial to an understanding of communication as an active process. Feedback refers to messages listeners send to speakers, which enable an analysis of the speakers' effectiveness. In its broadest terms, feedback is any information gained about the result of a communication process. Without feedback, it is not possible to know if one has been understood. Effective communication feedback is:

- Immediate (when possible)
- Honest
- Appropriate to the communication situation
- Clear and informative.

The following strategies, exercised by each participant in a meeting, will give feedback and contribute to creating an environment in which quality communication occurs:

Listen carefully.

Control defensive reactions, and instead keep track of questions
or disagreements to discuss later.

Paraphrase what others say to verify accurate understanding.

Ask questions for clarification.

Evaluate the value of what is said.

Do not overreact but, when desirable, modify behavior in suggested directions and evaluate the outcomes.[4]

Meeting participants can provide feedback either informally by reviewing and evaluating communication as it occurs or formally through techniques such as asking other participants at the end of the meeting for specific comments and suggestions related to their understanding of not only what the meeting accomplished but what the next steps are.

Active Listening

Meeting participants cannot communicate effectively unless they listen well. It is common for people to "tune out" parts of the meeting that do not interest them or to hear only what supports their point of view. Equally common is the tendency to chime in prematurely before the speaker has had an opportunity to complete his or her thoughts. Typical obstacles or barriers to effective listening are:

- Prejudging the information or the person communicating
- Rehearsing a response rather than listening
- Filtering out certain information—selective listening
- Doing all of the talking or frequently interrupting.

Instead, individuals need to make a conscious effort to actively listen. They may not come naturally, but listening skills can be improved by:

- Paying attention, listening for the total meaning
- Avoiding interrupting
- Avoiding judgment of others' ideas, opinions, feelings
- Paraphrasing what another has said in order to check understanding
- Asking open questions that act as invitations for clarification
- Encouraging the speaker by using eye contact, nods, etc.
- Not changing the topic prematurely.

Development of active listening skills contributes to quality interactions between people, and the meeting convener, by demonstrating a commitment to listen, can encourage others to listen as well. Because decisions are often made within tight time frames, meeting participants may not take the time to fully understand others' points of view. However, good listening skills are an essential ingredient to making informed decisions by exploring issues and various viewpoints fully.

Group Dynamics and Individual Roles

Meetings are essentially groups of individuals working together. The fundamental existence of interdependence is the single most important characteristic of group dynamics and roles. Functioning groups contain a number of similar characteristics.

Groups tend to take on a life of their own. The group identity or personality is a powerful force that regulates the behavior of individual members, especially to maintain and perpetuate the group identity. Sometimes this characteristic results in perpetuating a group whose purpose has been accomplished. Frequent evaluation of the purpose and effectiveness of working groups and committees ensures that needless perpetuation does not occur. Sometimes a "sunset" clause is helpful so that groups are fully aware at the onset that their work has a beginning and an end. The "sunset" clause is a clear statement of what activities and goals are expected of the group and when it will disband.

The flow, content, and accuracy of communication are affected by the degree to which group members exhibit certain attributes or roles or exercise influence over one another—the degree of status and prestige they possess. Some individuals bring a set of roles and attributes with them by virtue of their position, while attributes of others emerge during the process of group formation and development. Persons with higher status can more easily take command of the group and its discussion, while individuals with lower status or prestige will have difficulty making an impact on the group, regardless of who has the most relevant information or creative ideas to contribute to decisions or to solve problems.

The Individual's Role within the Group

The individual's role can shift and completely alter the outcome and quality of all types of meetings. In order for a group to achieve its goal two basic functions need to be balanced: accomplishing the task and maintaining communication in order to ensure that the task will be accomplished.[5] Not only do status, prestige, and the various roles assumed by individuals affect the balancing act, but these elements are constantly shifting and changing over time in groups or committees.

Everyone plays a variety of roles each day. These roles occur as a result of interaction in specific situations. Within the library organization librarians hold different roles, often simultaneously, such as:

Prescribed role: usually denotes position, such as reference librarian, head of cataloging, or director of the library. This role carries with it certain expectations not attributable to the position.

Earned role: bestowed on a librarian as the informal leader or spokesperson for a specific group or purpose. An articulate member of the reference department frequently called upon to provide the "reference" point of view is an example.

Functional role: usually designated in advance and includes meeting convener, participant, and neutral facilitator (see Chapter 2 for more detailed treatment of functional roles).

Meeting purpose determines which role or roles will affect outcomes. Prescribed roles are more significant in departmental meetings where the department head is, by definition, the leader of the meeting. Ascribed roles are important at meetings of working groups with specific goals, such as automating circulation, where the value of expertise is clear. Earned roles, such as long-term, respected librarian, or charismatic personality, become important in informal meetings where appointed leaders are not present. In all cases, people with prominent roles tend to do the greatest amount of talking. In order to achieve broad participation in meetings it is important for participants to recognize these roles when they inhibit communication and to manage them so that all participants are more productive.

Norms and Conformity

Norms identify ways in which people are expected to behave. They are shared agreements among a group of people regarding expected behavior. Librarianship as a profession shares with other professions certain norms that affect interactions of all types, including meetings.

Joseph Raelin highlights the normative dilemma of professionals in his book, *The Clash of Cultures: Managers and Professionals.* He notes that experienced professionals share a body of knowledge and will sometimes defend even obsolete aspects of this knowledge. Many professionals are isolated from their organization's clientele, resulting in an isolationist view of client needs, the primary focus of management. The professional may be unwilling to relax insistence on specialized procedures in order to maximize service. Isolationism can also culminate in a constant tension between standards and the organization's real goals.[6] Some professionals dislike participation in what they consider to be useless management techniques for problem-solving and planning, for example. Both of these may be considered a waste of time and not productive, but, in fact, can be effective techniques to improve results in meetings.

Certain shared professional norms within librarianship may actually act as barriers to effective and productive meetings. Professionals themselves often shy away from conflict or disagreement, assuming that it is bad. In addition, some professionals are so specialized that it can be difficult for them to see their work in terms of the overall organizational goals. To complicate matters, librarianship has undergone rapid change during the past decade resulting in sharply different sets of shared norms. One can no longer be sure if norms, both positive and negative, are common to a group of professionals who are called together for a specific purpose. Conformity, which occurs when there is agreement on norms, is not a given anymore.

What happens when norms are not shared by participants? In addition to professional training (similar for most librarians), work experience, cultural differences, and other factors contribute to whether or not norms will be shared. Whenever norms are not shared they must be mutually established so that within a meeting setting there will be understanding. This understanding can occur by clarifying the goal of the meeting and focusing on desired outcomes. It also is important to understand the following:

Norms are not established by groups for every situation.

Norms may apply to all or only some members of the group.

The level of acceptance of norms will vary.

The range of permissible deviation varies for each norm.[7]

When a participant does not conform to the established norms within a group, then a great deal of initial communication may be directed toward this participant in order to influence him or her. If no change occurs, eventually group members will tend to reject and isolate the person. More pressure is placed on individuals to conform in groups that meet on a long-term basis than in groups that meet only once or a few times.

Cohesiveness

Cohesiveness is the overall attraction that group members have to each other and their desire, therefore, to be seen as a group with one or more important purposes. The attractiveness of a group to an individual will depend on the extent to which the group and participation in the group satisfies certain needs of the individual. From cohesiveness develops a commitment to work together, to be successful. The degree of cohesiveness affects the quality of the group's interaction, and cohesive groups also are productive, at least in terms of the group's own agenda.

Communication in a cohesive group is more likely to be balanced and more valued among members. In order to improve commitment and quality communication, cohesiveness is a desired attribute. The more cohesive a group the more likely each individual will be committed to the group goals and therefore spend time and energy toward accomplishing the group goals even above personal ones.

Group Size

Group size is an important variable that affects the quality of communication and thus decision-making. Decisions requiring quick turnaround time or involving creative thinking may be done more productively by one person. A group, when working productively, can bring to the discussion more skills and perspectives than one individual, with the additional benefit of the evaluation of one another's ideas.

According to Brightman, three factors can help determine whether a group or one person should be the problem-solver: (1) the effectiveness of the leader as problem-solver—does the leader have sufficient information to make a decision; (2) subordinates' and peers' need for involvement in decision-making and potential resources they bring to a team—do they have critical information, can they develop critical thinking skills, and do they need challenges and involvement; and (3) the characteristic of the problem—well-structured problem with a short time frame where the manager has all necessary information is best solved alone. A group decision is appropriate if staff have critical information, the decision must be defended to senior management or a board, the problem is unstructured, or staff must implement the solution.[8]

Some effects of group size on the effectiveness of meetings follow:

The larger the group, the more likely it will be dominated by more aggressive members and quiet members will have decreased participation.

Smaller groups are faster and more accurate in responding to specific problems, while larger groups are superior on abstract problems.

Total number of ideas may be greater in larger groups.

In larger groups people may feel freer to express their own ideas and to reject ideas of other people. The larger the group and less concern with alienating people decrease inhibition.

In a large group, feedback declines. A loss in communication may occur and an increase in hostility may develop.

Groups should be as small as possible while still containing all the necessary skills and ideas needed to accomplish the group task. When a large group is needed to generate ideas, it can be subdivided into task groups to work on specific plans and actions. The guiding principle, though, should be that the group size should allow each participant to make contributions to the activity.

Power and Influence

Power and influence are part of the formal structure of the organization, but individuals can also achieve power who do not fill a certain position similar to ascribed and earned roles discussed earlier.

Power of group members affects communication in several ways. A greater amount of communication comes from the person who has or is perceived as having power. The direction of communication tends to be vertical, from the person in power to others, and from others to the person in power. Therefore, meeting participants who are perceived as holding power in the organization or within the group that is meeting may inhibit open discussion. Group members may hold back their contributions waiting for orders or making sure that they do not say something to contradict the person perceived as powerful.

Individual Personalities

The influence of personality is another reality in the effectiveness and final outcomes of meetings. Meeting facilitators and participants need to be aware of potential problem personality types and to use appropriate communication styles and strategies to modify such behavior so that it does not prove to be a barrier. Surprisingly some personality types usually thought of as positive can be problematic in meetings.

Mosvick and Nelson examine several personality constructs. Type A is defined as aggressive, competitive, impatient, and hard-driving, and type B represents the easy-going, relaxed, and sociable individual. In small group settings, type A tends to monopolize the conversation and get into arguments, but is usually a high achiever and when properly channeled can be productive. Type B is relatively noncompetitive in a meeting setting. A third personality type is the authoritarian who often uses power to control and direct people. The authoritarian is inflexible and, in a subordinate role, more inclined to be submissive and compliant. Although the authoritarian is comfortable in a hierarchical setting, he or she often has difficulty in matrix-type groups and is not very effective as the meeting convener because of an unwillingness to truly embrace participative decision-making by individuals of different status levels. The manipulator, another type, acts primarily out of self-interest and will focus on topics related to enhancement of his or her situation even though these topics may not be relevant to the discussion.[9]

Dealing with Disruptive Participants

Meeting conveners and facilitators are responsible for keeping a meeting on track, including controlling disruptive behavior in order to maintain fairness and a productive environment. All points of view should be given a fair hearing and those that disagree should be encouraged to speak. Meeting leaders also need to recognize the general reluctance among library professionals to disagree and help the group see the difference between destructive remarks and critical evaluation and discussion of the issues. At the same time, the facilitator has the responsibility to cope with those who may try, for their own ends, to derail the meeting. According to Greville Janner, these individuals may try to:

Avoid discussion of later agenda items by provoking prolonged arguments over earlier ones.

Rush important but controversial items so as to win without adequate or critical discussion.

Induce the facilitator to call on people on their side.

Interrupt or silence their opponents.

Force a vote they believe they will win or avoid one if defeat is expected.[10]

Other types of participants include time wasters who comment on every issue. The facilitator needs to cut these types off in a face-saving manner. Another challenge is the naysayer, who immediately comments that "it will never work." The facilitator should immediately ask others to comment to counter this statement. Silent participants are among the most pervasive. They can be drawn out by asking them directly for an opinion based on their experience. Other personalities commonly found in meetings include the nonparticipant who rarely speaks or contributes and the casual talker who wastes time on unrelated chatter or jokes and, while occasionally entertaining, is unproductive.

Meeting conveners and participants can use several strategies and communication styles to counteract nonproductive behaviors and keep the meeting on track toward its stated goal:

Remind the group of its goal, redirecting those who stray from the topic at hand.

Ask those who are not participating to answer specific questions.

Use nonverbal techniques such as direct eye contact to engage participation or be more emphatic.

While it is helpful to be aware of different personalities and how they may affect the quality of meetings, stereotypes of people or personality types may lead to misunderstandings, thus damaging open communication. The challenge in a meeting is for all participants to focus on the substance of what someone is saying and not the personality or style of the person speaking. It is necessary to differentiate between the personality of the contributor and their contributions in order to concentrate objectively on the content.

Decision-Making in the Group Setting

Most people consider decision-making as a rational, logical act. It can also be impulsive and without basis. While there is no sure method for making the best possible decisions, some processes work best for group decision-making. Group decision-making differs from individual decision-making in that many more interpretations of data or information contribute to the process. And, while each person involved in the process may feel that he or she is going through a similar set of steps to determine the best decision, in reality as many methods as individuals involved may exist, which can lead to time-consuming confusion and a lack of direction.

A first step in the process is defining the problem. The group should be directed to focus on a specific target. Carefully defining the problem within the appropriate context for all members of the group provides a solid start to the decision-making process. However, there are pitfalls to this apparently simple process. Too much time spent discussing background information related to the problem can quickly derail the most ambitious group. Other common mistakes include articulating the problem in terms of a solution or focusing on one narrow aspect of the problem rather than examining the situation in its entirety.

Problem-solving before identifying and examining the real problem goes on all the time. It happens quite often because librarians are rushed. It occurs because of the feeling that excellence is measured by an ability to give a quick response. And, too often, this pattern is reinforced because planning is not an activity that is sufficiently recognized or rewarded.

Once the problem has been defined, the group should determine if the problem can be solved by routine procedures already in existence or if the problem is unstructured and requires the group to break new ground. It wastes time to deal with routine matters in a complex way or to try to solve complex situations using inappropriate procedures just because they already exist.

Research studies on how decisions are made can help meeting leaders take the most appropriate approach for the situation at hand. Sauser discusses the benefits of injecting contrast in the group decision-making process. He has developed six techniques to use in deliberations before decisions are made:

Invite diverse viewpoints so that tunnel vision can be avoided.

Reward contrasting opinions rather than stifling them or prematurely determining that they do not work.

Explore carefully the nature of the problem so that all relevant facets can be clearly stated and understood.

Consider a variety of alternative solutions rather than considering just one or the first one that is discussed.

Challenge each proposed solution in a rigorous and evaluative manner.

Expose hidden doubts where private matters of concern can be aired.[11]

Effective group decision-making requires a clear determination of the meeting goal, a mutual understood definition of the problem in its broadest context. The meeting convener and participants should guard against rushing to a resolution prematurely without carefully articulating the problem and exploring as many alternative solutions as possible. A number of problem-solving techniques currently exist and provide disciplined ways of approaching the problem or decision (see Appendix B for a number of frameworks for problem-solving).

Conflict Resolution

Handling intragroup conflict is essential to a group's problem-solving success. Brightman discusses five ways to handle team conflict:

Competing: win-lose arguing where reluctant team members are steamrolled into agreement.

Avoiding: members fail to take a position and withdraw.

Accommodating: members are cooperative but not assertive in presenting a position, attempting to eliminate conflict, which results in ineffective solutions.

Compromising: members seek a middle ground between positions where the solution hopefully contains the best of each person's thinking in the group.

Collaborating: members confront disagreements openly to find the best solutions, and these solutions are not necessarily compromises.[12]

The collaborative approach is usually the best because it emphasizes listening to all points of view, defining areas of agreement and disagreement, and working hard to come to a solution based on logic rather than emotion. Conflict between members over issues that have nothing to do with the meeting topic such as reliving an old arguement should be controlled by the meeting convener. However, subject-relevant conflict should be encouraged so that the group can produce conclusions that are thoroughly debated and examined. This type of conflict is both healthy and desirable.

Meeting participants who can effectively balance agreement and conflict and pay sufficient attention to diverse viewpoints rather than too quickly embracing apparent agreement will be more successful in making high quality decisions. Injecting contrast can also develop the interplay between goal-directed, logical thinking and the more creative or divergent thinking. The group can look at possibilities as well as what they consider to be realities of the problem or connection with the problem.

Summary

The meeting environment is dynamic and based on interactive communication. Interpersonal characteristics and awareness combined with the circular process of sending, receiving, and interpreting messages, not to mention providing feedback, ultimately define the quality and results of meetings. If participants, and especially the meeting convener, take into account the variables in the communication process, it is possible to make informed judgments and provide appropriate guidance rather than allowing participants to become reactive rather than collaborative.

Notes

1. John Wright, "Look at Management - 2: Communication," *Management Accounting* (October 1983), 33.
2. Audrey Fisher and Donald G. Ellis, *Small Group Decision Making: Communication and the Group Process* (New York: McGraw-Hill, 1974).
3. Catherine Sheldrick Ross and Patricia Dewdney, *Communicating Professionally* (New York: Neal-Schuman, 1989), 23.
4. Phillip V. Lewis, *Organizational Communication: The Essence of Effective Management* (New York: John Wiley & Sons, 1987), 147.
5. Ross and Dewdney, *Communicating Professionally*, 141.
6. Joseph Raelin, *The Clash of Cultures: Managers and Professionals* (Boston: Harvard Business School, 1986), 107.
7. Marvin E. Shaw, *Group Dynamics: The Psychology of Small Group Behavior* (New York: McGraw-Hill, 1976), 251.
8. Harvey J. Brightman, *Group Problem-Solving: An Improved Managerial Approach* (Atlanta: Georgia State University, College of Business Administration, 1988), 5.
9. Roger K. Mosvick and Robert B. Nelson, *We've Got to Start Meeting like This: A Guide to Successful Business Meeting Management* (Glenview, Ill.: Scott, Foresman, 1987), 76.
10. Jerry W. Koehler, Karl W. E. Anatol, and Ronald Applebaum, *Organizational Communication*, 2nd ed. (New York: Holt, Rinehart & Winston, 1981), 32.
11. William I. Sauser, "Injecting Contrast: A Key to Quality Decisions," *SAM Advanced Management Journal* (Autumn 1988), 22–23.
12. Brightman, *Group Problem-Solving*, 14.

4

Alternatives to Traditional Meetings: New Methods of Collaboration

As more people have ready access to network communications, the number and size of electronic groups will expand dramatically. It is up to management to make and shape connections. The organization of the future will depend significantly not just on how the technology of networking evolves but also on how managers seize the opportunity it presents for transforming the structure of work.[1]

Traditional face-to-face meetings involve considerable time and effort. Finding a time when all participants can come together for a meeting can be a nightmare. Finding an appropriate room or setting for the meeting can sometimes present a problem. And, when the meeting is away from one's own town or city, participants have to travel to another location expending time and money. This chapter examines alternatives available to accomplish the purpose of meetings.

New technology makes it possible for individuals to meet in different ways—informing; creating shared responsibility for directions, priorities, and results; encouraging contributions of ideas, views, and opinions; and providing settings for training and staff development. Some methods, such as audio and video teleconferencing, have been available for years, but cost, accessibility, and quality have limited their usefulness until recently. Newer collaborative technologies including electronic mail and electronic conferencing are proving to be effective options to traditional face-to-face meetings. Additionally, these computer-based technologies help participants prepare and share information before face-to-face meetings and to conduct follow-up activities.

In addition to computer-based communication tools, other technologies can streamline the decision-making process for work groups. These systems, sometimes referred to as group decision support systems, actually guide individuals or groups through the decision-making and planning process. Data about a particular problem is fed into specially designed computer hardware and decision support software, which analyzes the data providing different alternatives or solutions using modeling techniques and logic. Other innovations such as networked electronic meeting facilities enable groups to write and brainstorm together because it is now possible to view, share, and jointly manipulate a document.

The challenge is to understand how the different meeting tools affect communication and working patterns and to select the best method or combination of methods depending on the desired results. This chapter examines alternative meeting methods and outlines some of the advantages and disadvantages of these technologies. Many examples related to the use of electronic conferences for meetings are taken from the authors' survey, referred to in this chapter as the Iowa survey. The survey was placed on seven library-related electronic conferences, and it elicited eighty responses from library professionals across the country.[2]

Electronic Mail

New technology has made possible several methods of group and one-on-one communication in libraries using electronic means of communication in combination with local and national networks. The convenience and timeliness of electronic mail communication make it an attractive tool for library professionals to use. The ability to converse with and respond to queries in a local, national, or international environment provides an immediate and efficient way of providing service. Additionally, library users who rely on electronic mail will increasingly expect library professionals to provide services via this means. Library users should be able to seek online reference assistance, request the purchase or delivery of documents via electronic mail, and generally communicate more efficiently with library professionals using electronic networks.

Use of these electronic systems of collaboration has increased exponentially during the late 1980s, certainly in libraries where the use of all kinds of electronic networks is widespread. And, as in other kinds of organizations, network use alters the fundamental nature of conversations between people. Research on electronic mail offers examples of where it can be effective in the workplace. The Iowa survey found several general uses of electronic mail by library professionals, including communication of information, coordination of activities such as scheduling, dissemination of information directed toward specialized learning, and maintaining and establishing professional relationships.

Electronic mail (or e-mail) refers both to actual mail received electronically and also to the system of transmission.[3] Capabilities of e-mail range from basic sending and receiving functions to a wide variety of complex options. Possible features include the ability to:

Receive and send information in electronic form

Forward and send messages to individuals

Forward and send messages to groups

Store and retrieve incoming and outgoing information

Revise or add to messages

Browse incoming messages.

Messages can be printed out in hardcopy or stored in a computer file where they can be reviewed electronically at any time. Electronic mail systems can be used internally only or networked on the national and international systems, such as Internet.

Electronic Mail and Meetings

Electronic mail therefore can be used as the actual meeting environment where members of a group or committee interact. E-mail is also used as a tool to support activities of traditional face-to-face meetings in the following ways:

Scheduling—meetings can be scheduled by querying participants to find mutually agreeable times.

Agenda distribution—agendas can be distributed by e-mail, thus eliminating the time delay and staff time required to prepare mailings.

Background material distribution—material needed for meeting preparation can be sent by e-mail.

Assignments—specific assignments can be sent over e-mail.

Status reports—updates on tasks and activities can be sent to meeting participants and others.

Polling—participants can be polled by e-mail for opinions and ideas.

Reminders—group leaders can send reminders about meetings and deadlines.

The Advantages of Electronic Mail

Electronic mail provides many advantages for individuals and groups including providing a kind of freedom because constraints of time and space are lifted. Additional advantages include the ability to:

Communicate at any time to others, even with those working on different shifts and in different physical locations.

Reduce transmission time, compared to traditional written communication.

Communicate throughout the organization in a less hierarchical manner.

Obtain wide input on issues by sending the message to many individuals at once.

Circulate messages to others interested in learning the same information.

Productivity generally increases with the use of electronic mail. According to Long, time savings in organizations using electronic mail averaged about 4 percent for managers and 6 percent for professionals as measured by work statistics, but actual productivity for the group involved in his study increased 10 percent.[4] In a study of personal computer-based electronic mail at a General Motors division, lateral communications increased and the use of electronic communication actually stimulated personal contact. Overall, the study demonstrated that the use of this technology was responsible for increases in organizational efficiency, effectiveness, creativity, and innovativeness.[5]

Of the library professionals queried in the Iowa study 89 percent indicated that electronic mail improved productivity in general in their work. An example of how e-mail increases productivity in libraries was described by Tom Wilding, associate director for administration, Massachusetts Institute of Technology Libraries. He notes that "in general, staff at all levels have managed to integrate electronic mail into their work lives and it has definitely led to more effective use of time and more effective communications. No longer does one have to wait to see someone to tell them something before it has slipped their mind. Electronic mail allows me as an administrator to inform the managers who report to me of important decisions within minutes of their being made."

Finholt, Kiesler, and Sproull found that individuals in groups using electronic mail increased both coordination and cohesiveness:

> Notice that we are referring not just to improved coordination of partitioned work, but to a group working in a new way, offloading more work onto parts of the group and using computer mail as an electronic link between individual activity and the group. By partitioning the work and keeping others informed, people would have greater control over and responsibility for their own work.[6]

An example from the Iowa survey supports this finding. Carolyn Anne Reid, Cornell University Medical Library, notes

> Time-saving communication is absolutely the most positive aspect. Even though we're a small staff and very close together physically (only 33,000 sq. ft. on two floors), trying to reach someone by phone or dropping by their office often takes a great deal of time. My regular practice now is to try the phone and then use e-mail (or, more and more, just use e-mail first). Just now, four of us engaged in an "almost real time" on-line conference about a policy issue and quickly (within 15 min., with about 10 messages back and forth) reached a decision of the best approach to follow. Another big advantage is day to evening and weekend staff communications. It's really easy now for the weekend supervisor to report facilities problems that administration can take care of

first thing Monday morning without worrying about lost paper notes, etc.

Electronic mail is not only a viable means for library professionals to reach decisions and share information but it also encourages new working relationships. A study conducted by Bikson and Eveland provides an example of the way the structure of working relationships change with electronic communications. They looked at how two task forces in a large utility firm examined employee retirement issues. One group worked on networked computer facilities and the other did not. Both formed subcommittees, but the networked group also organized its subcommittees in overlapping matrix structure, added new subcommittees, and involved retirees outside the organization. This electronic-based task force was more flexible and less hierarchical in structure than the other. Retirees, a group who typically would be left out of any decisions, were well connected.[7]

The use of electronic mail can enhance professional development by providing a new professional network in which to learn and communicate. Pat Ensor, coordinator, Electronic Information Services, Indiana State University Libraries, summarizes the experience of many library professionals actively using conferences stating that

> E-mail usage through BITNET has literally changed my life. The people I have contacted have helped to increase my national recognition and my professional opportunities. Once I called for information on a new service we were hoping to provide, and ended up doing an online/CD-ROM conference poster session and an article in *CD-ROM Professional*. I sent out reports on a conference I went to, and through this, 1.5 years later, I am a columnist for *Technicalities*, get my conference reports published there, and am on the editorial board. These are major examples, but there are others. I cannot overemphasize the effects of E-mail on my life.

Electronic mail systems also provide more access to information by more levels of organizational people depending on who has access to the electronic mail systems and networks. For example, in the Iowa survey one respondent noted that, "I am not allowed to go to conferences due to my lowly clerical position. However, this type of conferencing has allowed me to get in touch with others out there and discuss things that are important to us in our daily ILL tasks."

Another effect noted by researchers of networked organizations is that patterns of information-sharing change. Electronic groups provide a forum for sharing information that in the past never included employees in remote locations, groups of employees in different physical proximities, employees who work different shifts, or employees of a nonprofessional status. Broad employee access and participation may result in more information-sharing and thus greater potential for input into decision-making. In some circumstances social contact actually increases because of the ability to talk to others irrespective of temporary or physical constraints. This increase is certainly true for individuals in a library with more than one branch or several campuses.

Written electronic communication can be improved in several ways:

Design messages carefully to ensure that the meaning of electronic mail interchanges is clear.

Use a more natural and direct style of written communication, which is more effective than the traditional heavy and formal business writing of the past.

Use proper identification such as full name and telephone number so that the reader can contact the sender.

Disadvantages of Electronic Mail

Electronic mail systems also have certain disadvantages, which should be taken into consideration when determining whether and how to use e-mail for meetings or meeting support. Some negative characteristics include:

Messages so vague they initiate an incorrect reaction

Inability to restate or clarify an electronic message (as one would in face-to-face communication) where no verbal clues enhance an exchange

Discouragement of face-to-face communication

Limited effectiveness if few people in an organization have access to the system

Concern about confidentiality of messages, thereby eliciting mistrust among its users.

In a Carnegie Mellon study researchers investigated how small groups made decisions using computer conferences, electronic mail, and face-to-face discussion. This study found that using electronic mail or computer conferences took about four times as long to reach a decision as traditional meetings.[8] One of the Iowa survey respondents noted "often, because of rapid communication, I find work has to be done over and over again because it was not thought out clearly the first time. Additionally, the lines of communication are blurred, messages often sent to people who should not receive them and time is wasted on issues which were improperly communicated."

In addition, electronic modes of communication encourage what is known as flaming. In flaming, a participant uses strong language or sentiment in an electronic discussion. Written memos with this language are usually edited or discarded before being sent, whereas electronic messages tend to be sent immediately after their creation with a simple keystroke and without editing. Such emotional messages may create a barrier to communication and collaboration. However, at times they may allow controversial ideas and points of view to surface.

In addition, certain aspects of productivity can be limited by the way individuals use electronic mail. Overuse or even "addiction" causes people to spend more and more time on the system to the detriment of other duties and responsibilities. Judith Hopkins, technical services research and analysis officer, SUNY, Buffalo, noted in the Iowa survey that "I am afraid my use of e-mail conferences has had negative effects on my productivity. I subscribe to a large number of lists and forward messages of interest to my nonsubscribing colleagues but this is very time-consuming. List reading is addictive!" The time element is illustrated by an example from a recent message on a music library computer conference. It related the story of a librarian whose manager refused to allow him to use the conference because the manager felt it was a waste of time, although it contained up-to-date information on music librarianship, some of which could be applied in the local setting.

An Iowa survey respondent indicated that electronic mail can extend the problems created by ineffective management style:

In my present organization, there are some negative factors related to our director who uses in-house e-mail as an extension of
her crisis management style. She expects all staff members to be
at her beck and call and e-mail allows her to do this all day long;
also, she is a poor communicator in general so her messages are
often unclear and time is wasted in many instances.

Advantages overwhelm disadvantages when it comes to using
electronic mail. The freedom to communicate without regard to
time or physical location is valued by e-mail users. The ability
to send a variety of messages supporting a project simultaneously
to a work group is tremendously valuable. Access to information
and the opportunity for input throughout the organization are increased and cut across position lines. Productivity increases because
of the efficiency and speed of this type of communication. Not only
is electronic mail valuable for communicating with one person or
meeting with several, it also provides an avenue for professional development and collaboration. Although electronic mail does have
some disadvantages, they can be minimized if individuals exercise
discipline in their participation on electronic conferences and are
sensitive to how they respond to issues.

Computer Conferences and Bulletin Boards

Electronic conferences and bulletin boards allow messages to be
transmitted to a single mailbox that is accessible to more than one
person. Bulletin boards allow users to read and post messages for
everyone to receive. They differ from electronic mail, which is more
like a private conversation. Typical messages for bulletin boards are
relatively short and there is little interaction between users.

Computer conferences allow participants to send and immediately receive messages related to or in response to the theme of
the conference. It is possible to have a dialogue with one or more
participants in real time if both parties are using the system at the
same time. Conferencing systems can be operated within a library
where participants interact with each other on topics of interest in
their local environment as well as conferences that operate nationally. Conferences allow many participants at once to discuss issues
of common interest. These systems differ from standard electronic

mail because they provide shared files that users can read or contribute to, and are available to all participants.

Computer conferences are becoming an important method of communication among library professionals. Conferences provide an opportunity to ask questions about issues or answer others' queries, and more generally to contribute ideas on a particular issue. There are currently over forty-five different conferences on library-related topics available over Bitnet or Internet, the networks most commonly available to library professionals.[9] Library-related conferences provide a way for library professionals to explore issues related to serials, interlibrary loan, information/reference services, library planning, and music librarianship to name a few (see Appendix C, "Library-Oriented Computer Conferences," for a more complete list). For example, Charlotte Derksen of the Earth Sciences Library, Stanford University Libraries, reports that geology library professionals use computer conferences to obtain answers to reference questions, determine location of hard-to-find items, obtain prices and addresses for vendors, and notify colleagues of new products and duplicate materials.

John Waiblinger, assistant university librarian for academic information services, University of Southern California, reads electronic conferences related to the field of automation, before reading printed literature, to keep up-to-date. Janet Swan Hill, assistant university librarian for technical services, University of Colorado comments,

> E-mail is a virtual cocktail party at which general, specific, and philosophical issues are intertwined in the way they are face-to-face. There is no interrupting. When we discuss things locally, we don't often get into philosophy and ethics, but we should. E-mail provides this opportunity (sometimes it even forces it).

Conferences provide an opportunity for committee members from different locations to meet. Darren Meahl, head of systems, Michigan State University, provides the following example:

> While chair of the NOTIS Circulation Special Interest Group, I was able to correspond with the Steering Committee exclusively via e-mail. Since reaching any one of us by phone is next to impossible, e-mail made the Steering Committee actually able to accomplish real work instead of wasting time trying to reach each

other. Also, the minutes, meeting agendas, and enhancement proposals were distributed via e-mail, saving postage, and decreasing turnaround time for comments on proposals. I can't imagine how I (or any of my colleagues) managed a national committee before e-mail conferencing!

Other electronic conferences exist with the potential for linking library professionals to researchers in disciplines ranging from American literature to science fiction. The Association of Research Libraries publishes the *Directory of Electronic Journals, Newsletters and Academic Discussion Lists*. It is a compilation of entries of 800 scholarly lists, 80 newsletters, and 17 other titles, and it includes specific instructions for electronic access. One section lists, by subject, computer conferences in which extensive meetings are held on a daily basis.[10] Subject-based computer conferences enable library professionals to collaborate regularly with scholars contributing solutions to issues of interest related to all disciplines. Conferences, therefore, allow participants not only to choose the topic and group they are interested in, but to determine each time they log on whether or not to contribute or to simply take away relevant information. And, communication is all done on a timetable determined by the conference participant.

Advantages of computer conferences include:

- Ability to target topics by issue or interest
- Connection with large numbers of individuals with similar interests
- Ability to bring ideas from physically remote locations to an organization directly.

Some disadvantages of computer conferences follow:

- Time lag for replies to queries
- Lengthy and time-consuming content of chosen conference
- Confusing multiple threads to a discussion due to lack of organized "turn-taking."

Conferences provide library professionals with the opportunity to meet and interact with others with similar interests. Conferences enable professionals to keep up with the latest developments and trends as well as providing an opportunity to share their expertise with others.

The Telephone and Voice Mail

Use of the telephone for conducting meetings is covered in Chapter 1. Voice mail, on the other hand, is a computer-aided telephone system capable of storing and forwarding digitized spoken messages. These systems offer a wide range of benefits and applications compared to traditional telephone communication and are sometimes connected to electronic mail systems. Voice mail assists individuals who need to meet with one other person and also provides meeting conveners with yet another way to distribute agendas and background materials.

There are two categories of voice mail—voice answering and voice messaging. Voice answering is the interception, receipt, and storage of messages for the receiver to review at his or her convenience. The receiver then responds to the message in whatever format seems appropriate (memo, telephone, electronic mail, etc.). Voice answering is particularly appropriate for tasks characterized by:

- Large volume of phone calls, especially when concentrated during one time of the day
- Predictable messages
- The need to capture routine information without providing feedback.[11]

Voice messaging is the intentional use of the system for processing the communication such as forwarding, distribution lists, prioritizing, speed browsing of messages, etc. Similar to electronic mail, it is appropriate for organizations where:

Exchanging information among a group of employees is frequent.

Persons who are hard to reach because of their schedule or physical proximity are involved.

Information needs to be stored for future delivery.

Advantages of voice mail include:

More information can be received than through traditional answering machines.

Situational constraints are reduced.

Activities can be coordinated when there is sufficient mass of other users.

Voice mail use leads to improved ability to distribute and obtain information.

Two disadvantages of voice mail are that:

It requires a critical mass of participants in the organization to be successful.

The technology can be expensive.

Using telecommunications technology in the form of the ordinary telephone or in the more technologically sophisticated form of voice mail is often an option to the face-to-face meeting. While not appropriate for highly sensitive issues, many problems and decisions can be solved using telephonic means.

Electronic Meeting Facilities—Group Decision Support Systems

Group decision support systems "combine communication, computer, and decision technologies to support the decision-making and related activities of work groups."[12] According to Long these methods are either content-oriented or process-oriented.[13] Content-oriented systems are designed to solve a specific problem. The system specifies to the user what information must be input, then it arrives at a programmed decision or solution based on that information. Expert systems are content-oriented. Process-oriented systems provide mechanisms to facilitate the decision-making process either for an individual or for groups of people.

Decision-enhancing systems vary tremendously in their cost and complexity ranging from a single personal computer to a multi-station computerized meeting environment. These systems usually fall within two categories.

In the single personal computer system, decision support software leads an individual user or group through a set of queries, prioritizes their answers, and indicates a direction or solution. In a multiple personal computer system, a highly sophisticated network is set up as an electronic meeting room.

Group decision support systems can integrate the use of group problem-solving methods with modified computer equipment and software in specially designed electronic meeting rooms. The electronic meeting room provides the potential for improved collaboration between participants, resulting in an immediate product. The meeting is turned into what Shrage terms "a genuine act of creation," which is shared. Work is actually accomplished. A technique DeKoven terms the *C-Cycle* is used to structure electronic meetings: (1) collect comments, (2) connect them, and (3) correct them.[14] A computer screen is used as a shared space providing a new environment for groups to solve problems, create innovations, and make decisions. (See Appendix C for techniques for using electronic meeting facilities.)

According to Finley, vendors of electronic meeting rooms and equipment claim that their systems can:

> Keep meetings and training sessions on track and focused on achieving the main objectives.
>
> Eliminate distractions.
>
> Stimulate new ideas and lively discussion.
>
> Ensure democratic involvement.
>
> Reduce number of meetings and save time.
>
> Help subdue strong personalities.[15]

Other advantages noted by users of the electronic meeting facility are:

> It works well with diverse groups of people.
>
> It provides a quicker process than traditional concensus-based methods.
>
> It allows a group to think, see, react, and rethink in quick succession.

Electronic meeting environments have some disadvantages. They include:

The system is technically difficult to use.

Facilitators trained in "traditional" methods sometimes have difficulty in learning the systems.

Multiple interacting issues are difficult to consistently deal with.

Decision-making processes may take longer.

Leaders who have control over the screen may inhibit the free flow of ideas.

As with all meetings, the group needs to be carefully chosen and must be willing to participate and work in a collaborative environment, sharing ideas and opinions freely. Although the group may not be entirely comfortable with all aspects of the process, it needs to trust it in order to achieve results.

Electronic meeting facilities are probably not readily available to most libraries, but some of the problem-solving equipment and devices used in these facilities are available to use on a single computer. Decision support systems can benefit those groups making decisions or solving problems requiring analysis of data combined with a more structured approach.

Video Conferencing

Video conferencing is full-motion, live video transmission. It can be a one-way broadcast from a single site to multiple remote sites, or a two-way interactive broadcast. Additionally, a video conference can consist of a one-way video broadcast with a two-way audio capability. Video conferencing technology has typically been too expensive and cumbersome for most organizations, and it does require physical space to house the sophisticated transmission equipment. However, recent technological developments are making this option more attractive.

According to a 1991 article in *Chronicle of Higher Education*, fully equipped video conference rooms, costing about $125,000 in the late 1980s, can now be assembled for about $50,000. Equipment for this new generation of interactive video conferencing technology includes two monitors with compression devices, an audio system, two cameras, a graphics stand, and a personal computer with interactive graphics for two different sites.

The new compressed digital video technology allows images and sound to be converted to computerized transmissions and sent over phone lines to remote locations, where they are converted back into images and sound, allowing for much less distortion than in the past. Such systems are now in place in Texas and Arizona providing institutions of higher education with more than one campus a more timely and economical means to communicate. Texas A&M uses a video conferencing system to allow participants at as many as fourteen sites to meet face-to-face. Arizona State University uses a video system to reduce travel costs between its two campuses.[16]

Advantages of video conferencing include:

- More task-oriented meetings
- Less hierarchically organized and status-oriented meetings
- Ability to use graphics and visual materials
- More equal participation.

Successful video conferencing, as with all meeting environments, requires careful planning and is not the answer for every type of meeting. Guidelines for effective implementation of a successful video conference include:

Agenda and predetermined goals should be focused and fairly brief.

One individual should be in charge of the meeting to make sure participants are moving through the agenda.

Technical assistance must be readily available during the conference.

The conference must be planned in advance so that participants are in place.

Participants must have all necessary materials needed for the conference in hand and must be prepared.

Someone must be responsible for follow-up to ensure that the conference's goals and plans are acted upon.

Video conferencing is an attractive alternative to face-to-face meetings because it has the ability to simulate electronically the feeling of actually being with the meeting group, but it also has the advantages of other electronic communication techniques including ease of scheduling and elimination of travel time. Video conferencing is becoming more available as costs go down and equipment is simplified, and thus, may be more common in libraries in the near future.

Computer-Assisted Meeting Management and Record-keeping

In traditional meetings, minutes are usually recorded and archived in some way depending on the importance and nature of the meeting. A recorder is generally selected in advance with the ability to clearly articulate the main points of the meeting. Meeting conveners need to determine when archiving is appropriate and in what format. Additionally, meeting conveners need to determine when it is appropriate to summarize meeting results and who will accomplish this.

Electronic means of archiving is available directly on some electronic bulletin boards and conferences. In this case messages are stored on the central computer housing the electronic mail system. Messages can also be kept on diskettes or in hard copy and stored. Recorders should consider using portable notebook computers at meetings to take minutes that can later be polished and archived in paper or electronically.

As was noted earlier, electronic communication can contain unrevised messages that may need editing prior to archiving. Also, the sheer volume of interchange may be too much to keep and a series of messages indicating the decisions resulting from the meeting may suffice. In any case, the convener must determine the process for record-keeping and archiving results of meetings.

Alternative methods of meeting require careful attention to recording and archiving results in order to achieve desired goals including necessary follow-up. New technologies such as electronic data storage and videotaping are options for recording and archiving meeting results in addition to or in place of written documentation.

Consequences of Technology: Organizational and Social

In order to select from among the many choices available for the exchange of ideas and for making decisions, library managers need to be familiar with possibilities and consequences the computer-based communication technology can have on the library organization. Shrage notes in *Shared Minds: The New Technologies of Collaboration* that "technology is really a medium for creating productive environments. As an organizational medium, technology is at its most expressive and powerful in the form of tools that build these productive environments."[17] The collaborative computing and communication technologies have, according to Sproull and Kiesler, both first-level or technical efficiency effects and second-level or social pattern effects:

> First-level effects of communication technology are the anticipated technical ones—the planned efficient gains or productivity gains that justify an investment in new technology. . . . Second-level effects from communication technologies came about primarily because new communication technology leads people to pay attention to different things.[18]

New technologies enable people to interact with others throughout the organization and with individuals external to the library. In addition, more professionals have direct access to organizational information where in the past they had to ask others for the information or simply did not have access. These changes in interdependence among professionals are fundamental and ultimately affect the organizational structure of the workplace itself. While electronic mail systems might be chosen, for example, to provide a more efficient way to communicate, organizations must take into consideration how this method or any of the other examples mentioned changes interaction, how this interaction plays out, how the interaction translates into results, and finally, how it may eventually change the structure of the workplace itself.

Zuboff notes that "the electronic text displays the organization's work in a new way. Personal sources of advantage depend less on private knowledge than upon developing mastery in the interpretation and utilization of the public electronic text."[19] Today many library professionals take full advantage of communication networks. However, those without access to or knowledge about electronic sources of information are at a disadvantage because they are out of touch in what is increasingly a primary method of keeping up with developments in the profession. It will be more and more difficult for them (and there are fewer each year) to move forward, even in their own specializations, because of this knowledge gap.

The use of alternative technologies for communication and collaboration has social and organizational implications. Library organizations, like society, have become more complex and information-reliant. Consider how the structure of jobs has changed because of the implementation of library automation systems. Activities previously performed by library professionals are now being accomplished by support staff. Library professionals have learned through this experience that it is necessary to rely on specialists to keep these systems updated and fully functional. The project approach to accomplishing goals requires that library professionals possessing different expertise come together to share knowledge and solve problems. Collaborative work groups are formed using electronic communications technology (such as conferences and electronic mail). Therefore the ability to select and make appropriate use of these new collaboration tools requires not only knowledge of the various technologies but also how they affect interactions and results of the working groups.

Attitudes toward Technology

Meeting conveners and library managers need to stress that the technology is meant to support collaborative efforts and recognize that some participants view certain tools with caution. However, given the large number of library-related listservs and the increasing number of participants on them. enthusiasm to use these tools is the most likely reaction.

The Clash of Cultures eloquently describes the tension inherent between professionals and management. The author notes that professionals tend to practice specialized competencies and to serve professional interests to the exclusion of organizational considerations. Technical expertise rather than other competencies is what professionals value, reinforced by common educational background and by professional activities.[20] Topic-focused listservs and conferences are an ideal communication vehicle for the specialized professional librarian and are therefore becoming a part of the professional culture of librarianship.

The Iowa survey results contain numerous examples of positive ways in which library-related conferences are used. Of the eighty library professionals responding to the survey (most were from different institutions), sixty-five indicated that electronic conference participation provides a timely way to stay current on issues in their specific area of specialization. Successful implementation of these systems is more likely if administrators recognize the need for training and direction on the value of actually using the systems effectively once training has occurred. Professionals need to understand that methods of electronic communication require a commitment by them to try out the new methods and apply them to appropriate uses.

Summary

Computer-mediated communication and group work are a winning team. Time and distance considerations are no longer barriers to using the team approach. Technologies for collaborative work eliminate some of the coordination and group integration concerns because they create new work structures. Participation through the network has literally connected entire communities of experts with others who need answers to their questions. As one librarian in the survey said, "It has expanded our networks and people-resources immensely." At the local level these systems have dramatically increased access to information and sometimes input into decision-making because more people are in the loop.

Of course, appropriate application of these systems to organizational group work is necessary for maximum effectiveness and productivity. Maximum accessibility for as many staff as possible is an obvious prerequisite to success. Attention to training coupled with the librarian's willingness to adjust to these new collaborative technologies is essential. It is important to understand that these methods can also supplement face-to-face meetings as well as enhance such meetings. The application of these systems in combination with team-based, project-oriented work environments will, in time, transform how library professionals provide service in the information age.

Notes

1. Lee Sproull and Sara Kiesler, "Computers, Networks and Work," *Scientific American* 265 (September 1991), 91.
2. Sheila D. Creth and Barbara I. Dewey, "The Iowa Survey" unpublished survey on electronic mail usage sent to the following listservs in spring 1992: Circulation and Access Services, Interlibrary Loan, Library Administration and Management, Library Reference Issues, Public-Access Computer Systems Forum.
3. Jacqueline Robinson, *Collaborative Computing Work Groups* (University of Tasmania: Department of Sociology, unpublished M.A. thesis, 1991), 3.4.
4. Richard J. Long, *New Office Information Technology: Human and Mangerial Implications* (London: Croom Helm, 1987), 70.
5. L. W. Foster and D. M. Flynn, "Management Information Technology: Its Effect on Organizational Form and Function," *MIS Quarterly* 8:4 (1984): 229–36.
6. Tom Finholt, Lee Sproull, and Sara Kiesler, "Communication and Performance in Ad Hoc Task Groups," in Jolene Galegher, Robert E. Kraut, Carmen Egido, eds., *Intellectual Teamwork: Social and Technological Foundations of Cooperative Work* (Hillsdale, N.J.: L. Erlbaum Associates, 1990), 295.
7. T. K. Bikson and D. Eveland, *Implementation of Office Automation* (Santa Monica: Rand Corporation, 1984), 5.
8. Sproull and Kiesler, "Computers, Networks and Work," 87.
9. Charles W. Bailey, Jr., "Library Oriented Conferences and Electronic Serials," Public-Access Computer Systems Forum (PACS-L@UHUPVM1.BITNET), January 3, 1992.
10. Association of Research Libraries, *Directory of Electronic Journals, Newsletters and Academic Discussion Lists* (Washington, D.C.: Association of Research Libraries), 1991.
11. Jolene Galegher, Robert E. Kraut, and Carmen Egido, eds., *Intellectual Teamwork: Social and Technological Foundations of Cooperative Work* (Hillsdale, N.J.: L. Erlbaum Associates, 1990), 330.
12. Marshall S. Poole and Geraldine DeSanctis, "Understanding the Use of Group Decision Support Systems: The Theory of Adaptive Structuration," in James Fulk and Charles Steinfield, eds., *Organizations and Communication Technology* (Newbury Park, Calif.: Sage, 1990), 173.

13. Long, *New Office Information Technology*, 106.
14. Michael Schrage, *Shared Minds: The New Technologies of Collaboration* (New York: Random House, 1990), 128.
15. Michael Finley, "Welcome to the Electronic Meeting," *Training* (July 1991), 31.
16. Katherine S. Mangan, "Colleges Use Video Conferences to Trim Their Travel Budgets," *Chronicle of Higher Education* 38 (December 11, 1991), A19.
17. Schrage, *Shared Minds*, 67.
18. Lee Sproull and Sara Kiesler, *Connections: New Ways of Working in the Networked Organization* (Cambridge, Mass.: MIT Press, 1992), 4–5.
19. Shoshana Zuboff, *In the Age of the Smart Machine* (New York: Basic Books, 1988), 35.
20. Joseph Realin, *The Clash of Cultures: Managers and Professionals* (Boston: Harvard Business School Press, 1986), 107.

Advance Planning and Physical Arrangements

The success of meetings begins with the advance preparation for all aspects of the meeting itself from the agenda through the arrangement of the meeting room. The time invested in advance planning will be well worthwhile when the participants come together because they will benefit from a well-organized and focused meeting.

In this appendix, the reader will find the Meeting Planner's Checklist, which provides an excellent reference for every aspect of conducting an effective meeting. In addition, the Meeting Action Plan is also included to suggest a framework for recording the actions that result from a meeting.

The physical arrangements for a meeting is another component that should be given careful thought because the environment can limit or restrict participation or enhance it; at the very least, the meeting location should have a neutral effect on the quality of the meeting. Guidelines for room arrangement and equipment also appear in this appendix.

Room arrangements should be determined based on the objective for the meeting. If a great deal of interaction is required among the participants, then the positions of tables and chairs should encourage a free flow of conversation by having everyone seated where they can see and be seen by everyone else. There should be sufficient space for individuals to sit comfortably with the materials they need easily at hand. And, finally, all participants should have a clear sightline to any materials that are presented on a screen or board. The materials on various room arrangements should assist a meeting planner in determining the most appropriate arrangement for each situation.

Meeting Planner's Checklist

For right reasons, participants, agenda

1. What is the purpose of this meeting?

   a) Explain a plan or project

   b) Tell people what to do...and how

   c) Report on what's been done

   d) Gain support for an idea

   e) Define or solve a problem

   f) Gain consensus for a decision

   g) Training

   h) Motivation

2. Is this meeting really necessary? Could I accomplish its purpose more effectively by:

   a) Phone call or teleconference?

   b) Sending a memo?

   c) Meeting one-on-one with those involved?

3. Have I invited the right people?

   a) Those in a position to contribute?

   b) The decision-makers?

   c) Those responsible for implementation?

4. Have I invited the right number of people?

   a) Problem identification: 10 or fewer

   b) Problem-solving: 5 or fewer

   c) Training: 15 or fewer

   d) Motivation: Unlimited

   e) Information-sharing: Only those who really need to be there

5. Have I prepared an agenda?

6. Have I allowed enough time?

7. Am I prepared?

For the right room

1. How many people will attend?

2. What kinds of visuals and equipment will I be using?

3. Will I be displaying product, and is there enough space to do that?

4. Will there be any kind of demo, and is there enough space to do that?

5. What type of room set-up should I have?

   a) U-shape

   b) Classroom

   c) Center table

   d) Auditorium

   e) Other

6. Have I made my room reservation?

7. Am I positive that the room I've reserved is right for my meeting, or should I check it out personally?

   a) Is it appropriate to the size of the group?

   b) Too small, too big, or just right?

   c) Will participants have a clear view of my visuals?

8. Do I need food service?

For the right equipment

1. What kind of equipment do I need?

2. Will I operate it myself, or would it be better to have a technician do it?

3. If I decide to operate it myself, am I really thoroughly familiar with its operation?

4. If showing a videocassette, what kind of VCR do I need? Should it be for beta, VHS, or U-Matic 2?

5. If I'm using film, do I need a 16 mm, 8 mm, or Super 8 mm projector?

6. If I am using the LCD for presenting, have I allowed enough room next to my overhead projector to put my PC?

7. Have I allowed enough time for equipment set-up before the meeting?

8. Is the equipment I'm going to use compatible with the room I've reserved?

9. Suppose I have an equipment problem? Do I have a phone number handy to call for help?

For the right visuals

1. What kinds of visuals will I be using at my meeting?
   a) Easel pad
   b) Overhead transparencies
   c) Slides
   d) Liquid Crystal Display Panel
   e) Videocassette
   f) Motion picture
   g) Charts
   h) Hand-outs

2. Do I have the necessary lead time to get those visuals produced?

3. Can I produce the visuals myself or will I need outside help?

4. Is the sophistication of the visuals appropriate to the audience?

5. What kinds of slides or overheads will I need to make my presentation most effective?
   a) Photos
   b) Artwork
   c) Copies
   d) Title and text charts
   e) Table charts

f) Bar charts
g) Line charts
h) Pie charts

6. Are my visuals uncluttered and easy to understand?

7. Do I have them in logical sequence?

8. Will they be back in time to permit me to rehearse?

For the right skills

1. Honestly evaluate your meeting leadership skills:
   a) What are my strong points? My weak points?
   b) How effective was I at the last meeting I called?
   c) What did I do well? Poorly?
   d) What can I do to improve?
   e) Would I benefit from additional training?

2. Do I customarily rehearse for my meetings?

3. Am I really good at encouraging participation? Do I get full value from what participants have to contribute?

4. Do I know how to control troublesome participants without creating a confrontation?

5. Do I customarily consult my agenda so that both I and the participants know where we are in the meeting process?

6. Do I usually summarize at various key points during the meeting?

7. Do I make effective use of visuals?

8. At the end of my meetings, is it clear as to what has been accomplished and what is to happen as a result?

The Checklist appears here courtesy of 3M Visual Systems Division.

Meeting:_____

Meeting date:_____ Recorder:_____

Meeting Action Plan

Chair:

Action to be taken	Person responsible	Deadline	Completed

Key issues or discussion

_____
_____
_____
_____
_____
_____
_____
_____
_____
_____
_____
_____

List attendees attached   Time: End:_____

                                       Start:_____

Next meeting:_____   Length:_____

ROOM AND EQUIPMENT ARRANGEMENT

Projector Arrangement

In the accompanying illustrations, the speaker and projector are placed in a standard position. However, the screen is in the corner at an angle so the speaker won't obstruct the view of some participants.

When you place the screen at an angle, it is preferable for the screen to be 40 degrees or less. Most screens can perform well within this range. A white matte screen with keystone eliminator is a good choice.

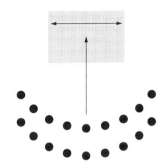

The 6 x rule. The distance of the audience from the screen should be no more 6 times the width of the projected image.

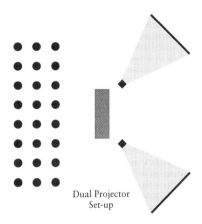

Dual Projector Set-up

Dual Overhead Projectors

Dual projectors can be used in several of the room arrangements shown here. The major advantage is that this arrangement allows the presenter (or sometimes two presenters) to introduce a series of key points on one screen while using the second screen to show details of the key points.

Room and Equipment Arrangement appears here courtesy of 3M Visual Systems Division.

Viewing Distances

Visuals, by definition, are meant to be seen. When they can't be seen, one of two things has gone wrong. Either the projected image is too small or the audience is too far from the screen. Same difference.

Most often, confused visuals result when people put too much information on their slides or overheads…too many numbers or words on charts or lists. Here are some rules of thumb that can prevent this from happening to you.

Overhead Transparencies

Checkpoint One: You should be able to read everything from a distance of 10 feet.

Checkpoint Two: The distance of the audience from the screen should be no more than 6 times the width of the projected image (The 6 x Rule). Example: If your image is 4 feet wide, the audience should be within 24 feet of the screen.

ROOM AND EQUIPMENT ARRANGEMENT *(continued)*

Slides

Checkpoint One: If the original artwork from which the slide was prepared can be read from a distance 8 times its height, you can expect it to be legible when projected.

Checkpoint Two: Follow the 6 x Rule as above.

Office Meeting Room

Office Meeting Room

In small offices that lack a conference table, the best approach when using visuals is to set up a desktop overhead projector at one end of the desk. The speaker stands behind the desk and projects onto a screen (or light-colored wall) behind him or her. This works fine for a group no larger than 6.

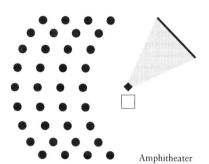

Amphitheater

Amphitheater

This is the very best setting for presentations of short to moderate length. Here, the audience sits on elevated levels in half circles round the speaker. This configuration permits the seating of more people per square foot of floor space than other arrangements and yet puts everyone relatively close to the presenter. In a well-designed amphitheater, acoustics are remarkably good, and the entire audience will have a clear view of the speaker and the projection screen. The amphitheater is ideal for presentations followed by a question and answer session. However, because of the rather limited space per person, it's not recommended for long meetings or those requiring work space for the participants.

Techniques for Problem-Solving and Improving Staff Contributions

The techniques outlined in this appendix represent a few of the better known methods for problem-solving, but there are many other processes available. Also, the reader will want to refer to the cited works for more detailed descriptions of the methods and their uses. Included here are brief summaries primarily of the steps of the methods.

Both Chapter 2 and Chapter 3 describe the need for a framework for problem-solving and a process that will ensure broader contribution of ideas from those participating in a meeting. Groups approaching their work without a method in mind risk wasting time and ideas because of an inability to organize their collective energies and constructively develop and communicate ideas. The methods outlined require preparation and forethought, and participants will improve their ability to apply the methods with practice.

Delphi Method

Description

The purpose of the delphi method is to forecast future directions of a program or operation providing an opportunity for participants to develop objective but varied viewpoints. Because delphi groups are dispersed and anonymous, the process can often be used effectively via electronic mail. Participants work on the problem through written responses to a set of questions prepared in advance.

Advantages

- Face-to-face interaction is not part of the method so larger numbers of participants can be used as well as participants who are geographically dispersed.
- Anonymity of responses prevents interpersonal issues from inhibiting contributions of group members.
- The act of writing may force participants to think through their responses and ideas more thoroughly.
- Participants can work on their response at their convenience.

Disadvantages

- Distribution and collection of the responses can be time-consuming, though time can be saved using electronic mail.
- Some participants may be poor writers.
- Some participants may lose interest because activities are performed independently.

Steps

1. Topic or issue is formulated based on information needed to solve a problem.
2. Participants are selected.
3. Initial set of questions is developed, pretested, and sent to participants.
4. Results are analyzed.
5. Second set of questions is developed. They should summarize responses, seek written clarification, statements of agreement or disagreement, and request participants to prioritize responses.
6. Responses are then analyzed, tallied, and summarized.
7. Final report is circulated including original goals of the process, describing the procedure, and reporting the results.

From *Delphi*, by N. D. Dalkay (Chicago: Rand Corporation, 1967).

Nominal Group Technique

Description

The Nominal Group Technique provides a framework for all group members to become immediately involved working on a problem and suggesting ideas. The technique is based on research that shows that people produce more and higher quality ideas when working face-to-face in silence than working alone. The nominal group technique is useful for identifying elements of a problem or solution, or to set priorities for a solution.

Advantages

- Greater number of ideas and alternatives are produced.
- All members have a chance to contribute.
- Problems resulting from direct interaction are minimized.

Disadvantages

- The technique is too time-consuming for simple problems.
- The single question focus does not work well for a problem where several questions need quick answers.
- A skilled group convener is necessary.

Steps

1. Group members silently generate ideas to a posed question or problem.
2. Each group member in round-robin fashion orally presents one idea at a time.
3. Group convener reads in item order and asks for clarification; duplicate items are eliminated.
4. Members individually rank a number of top priority items. Convener collects and tabulates the priority lists.
5. Initial vote is discussed.
6. Final vote is taken.

From *Group Techniques for Program Planning: A Guide to Nominal Group and Delphi Processes*, by Andre L. Delbecq, Andrew H. Van de Ven, and David H. Gustafson (Glenview, Ill.: Scott, Foresman, 1975).

Creative Idea Formation (Brainstorming)

Description

During the last three decades researchers from various creativity institutes evolved elaborate formats for problem-solving. Creative idea formation, popularly known as brainstorming, was a breakthrough in the group processing of ideas because of its simplicity and broad potential for practical application. It is built on four basic steps.

Advantages

- Constraints are few, and therefore creativity is encouraged.
- Participation by traditionally "quiet" members is encouraged.
- Creativity process stimulated early in addressing a problem.

Disadvantage

- Entire group must play by rules of suspending judgment and opting for maximum creativity.

Steps

1. All evaluation or criticism of ideas is suspended.
2. The widest possible variety of ideas is encouraged.
3. Quantity, not quality, of ideas is the group goal.
4. Ideas built on those previously offered is encouraged.

From *We've Got to Start Meeting like This: A Guide to Successful Business Meeting Management,* by Roger K. Mosvick and Robert B. Nelson (Glenview, Ill.: Scott, Foresman, 1987); A. F. Osborn, *Applied Imagination* (New York: Scribner, 1957).

Wright's "494" Agenda

Description

The Wright "494" Agenda is basically a solution-oriented process including establishing criteria and selecting and implementing solutions. It is appropriate for one-time as well as ongoing meetings.

Advantages

- Format is comprehensive.
- Format is flexible.

Disadvantage

- Ten-step system might be too detailed, might take more time than necessary.

Steps

1. Ventilation—release of initial tension.
2. Clarification—clarify problem and establish group goals.
3. Analysis of problem.
4. Set general criteria or basic standards for needed solutions.
5. Suggest general approaches or solutions—may brainstorm here for typical solutions.
6. Evaluate solutions by general criteria and disregard those that don't meet criteria.
7. Develop more specific criteria appropriate for this particular problem.
8. Evaluate solutions by specific criteria.
9. Select best solution for the particular problem.
10. Implement solution.

From *Small Group Communication: An Introduction*, by D. W. Wright (Dubuque, Iowa: Kendall/Hunt, 1975).

Maier's Posting Format

Description

This is a method of comparing two or more competing ideas and proposed solutions. Group members list the prepared ideas or solutions and then suggest advantages and disadvantages for each. Finally, the group returns to an open discussion of the solutions in order to make the final choice. This technique can be combined

with Wright's "494" agenda technique to emphasize initial generation of ideas before evaluating them.

Idea A		Idea B	
Advantages	Disadvantages	Advantages	Disadvantages
1.	1.	1.	1.
2.	2.	2.	2.
3.	3.	3.	3.

Advantages

- Reduces polarization among group members.
- Forces individuals to see both sides of an issue.
- Helps convenor and the group manage competing ideas in a rational manner.

From *Problem-Solving Discussion and Conferences*, by Norman R. F. Maier (New York: McGraw-Hill, 1963).

PERT (Program Evaluation and Review Technique)

Description

PERT was originally a statistics-based method for systematically coordinating highly complex group decisions. The method tries to account for all critical steps in reaching a solution by starting with the finished product or desired goal and working back through assumptions and processes required to make the final goal happen. PERT is helpful in specifying how a solution is to be implemented and in double-checking all of the assumed or hidden decisions required before the final outcome can take place.

Advantages

- Forces a group to anticipate most efficient route including roadblocks to its goal.
- Encourages consensus on often forgotten intermediate steps.

- Encourages group understanding of the whole process.
- Enables group to plan to use resources efficiently in resolving bottlenecks.

Disadvantage

- Takes a good amount of time to follow all steps.

Steps

1. Goal or event to be accomplished is specified.
2. All events that must happen before final outcome are listed in a comprehensive, although perhaps not chronological, manner.
3. Events are ordered chronologically.
4. Specific activities are listed between each pair of events.
5. Time estimates and cost requirements are made for each activity, including the best and most likely times required for completion of each.
6. Completion times are calculated. Calculations are cumulated for entire project.
7. Feasibility of deadlines is determined.
8. Master plan, sometimes called the critical path, is determined.

From *Communication and the Small Group*, by G. M. Phillips (Indianapolis: Bobbs-Merrill, 1966).

Standard Agenda Performance System

Description

Standard Agenda Performance System (SAPS) emphasizes five steps that guide implementation of a desired solution and like PERT forces the group to consider the entire process before moving ahead.

Advantages

- Includes an evaluation for each step.
- Provides a means to clearly determine allocation of personnel and time for a project from beginning to end.

Disadvantages

- Group members need to be familiar with all aspects of a problem.
- Process works only if group members can work beyond the conceptual phase to the implemention phase.

Steps

1. Recognize and define the problem.
2. Establish criteria to evaluate solutions.
3. Analyze the cause of the problem.
4. Find solutions to the problem.
5. Select the best solution and test it.
6. Determine final objective and completion date.
7. List necessary tasks on a timeline.
8. Lay out diagram.
9. Complete each task.
10. Evaluate each task as it is completed.

From *We've Got to Start Meeting like This: A Guide to Successful Business Meeting Management*, by Roger K. Mosvick and Robert B. Nelson (Glenview, Ill.: Scott, Foresman, 1987).

Brainstorming in the Electronic Meeting Room

Description

A key element in the electronic meeting room is the shared screen or display that is normally placed centrally in front of participants seated at semicircular tables.

Process

An individual, other than the meeting leader, should be assigned to track the conversation and map it on the screen.

Use rotating scribes to allow people to take turns at the keyboard making their own contributions known.

Advantages

- Allows immediate visualization of participants' ideas to the entire group.
- Provides an efficient way of pulling ideas together with all participants viewing the process.
- Final outcome is a tangible printout that all participants can take with them visually indicating progress.

Disadvantages

- Technology can become a barrier if technical expertise is not immediately available to solve equipment problems.
- Participants who are comfortable and adept with the technology can try to take over the screen and therefore the meeting unless convener or facilitator controls this.
- Equipment must be purchased and facilities outfitted for this technique.

Steps

A combination of steps from standard brainstorming methodologies can be used.

1. Collect ideas.
2. Connect ideas—group, edit, connect.
3. Correct ideas—discuss merits of ideas, extract pros and cons.
4. Vote and rank—use software with a ranking or weighting function.
5. Print out the results. The most tangible product of an electronic brainstorming session is the printout, a tangible product of the session.

From *Shared Minds: The New Technologies of Collaboration*, by Michael Schrage (New York: Random House, 1990).

Library-Oriented Computer Conferences

The following compilation developed by Charles Bailey lists the wide variety of computer conferences of interest to librarians. These conferences allow librarians from different locations to meet and confer frequently on issues relevant to their work. The conferences provide a valuable means for professionals to learn and contribute on a regular basis. Because conferences are developed almost on a weekly basis, this list is not comprehensive.

Library-Oriented Computer Conferences and Electronic Serials by Charles W. Bailey, Jr.

Computer Conferences

Computer conferences are becoming an increasingly important form of communication for librarians. There are a growing number of computer conferences of interest to librarians on BITNET and Internet.

Most BITNET conferences utilize the Revised LISTSERV software, which was written by Eric Thomas. This software is referred to as the "list server." You can obtain a directory of LISTSERV documentation by sending the following e-mail message to any list server:

INFO?

Once you know the name of the desired documentation file, send another INFO command to the list server to obtain the file. For example, to get a file that describes searching the message database of a list, send the following command:

INFO DATABASE

Internet computer conferences use diverse software. Contact the person who sponsors the list you are interested in to get further information about how the conference software works.

Computer conferences on both BITNET and Internet are commonly called "lists."

1.1 BITNET Lists

Please note that some BITNET lists also have Internet addresses, which are not shown here.

ACRLNY-L@NYUACF	Listings of Library Jobs and Events
ADVANC-L@IDBSU	Geac Advance Library System
ALF-L@YORKVM1	Academic Librarian's Forum
ARCHIVES@INDYCMS	Archives and Archivists List
ARLIS-L@UKCC	Art Libraries Asssociation of North America
ATLAS-L@TCUBVM	Data Research ATLAS Users
AUTOCAT@UVMVM	Library Cataloging and Authorities Discussion Group
BI-L@BINGVMB	Bibliographic Instruction
BRS-L@USCVM	BRS/Search Users
BUSLIB-L@IDBSU	Business Librarians

CARL-L@UHCCVM	CARL Users
CDPLUS-L@UTORONTO	CDPLUS Software User Group
CDROMLAN@IDBSU	CD-ROM LANs
CHMINF-L@IUBVM	Chemical Information Sources
CIRCPLUS@IDBSU	Circulation and Access Services
CNI-ARCH@UCCVMA	Coalition for Networked Information Architecture and Standards Work Group
CNIDIR-L@UNMVMA	Coalition for Networked Information Working Group on Directories
CWIS-L@WUVMD	Campus-Wide Information Systems
ELEASAI@ARIZVM1	Open Library/Information Science Research Forum
ELLASBIB@GREARN	Library Automation in Greece
EXLIBRIS@RUTVM1	Rare Books and Special Collections Forum
FISC-L@NDSUVM1	Fee-Based Information Service Centers in Academic Libraries
GOVDOC-L@PSUVM	Government Documents
ILL-L@UVMVM	Interlibrary Loan
INFO+REF@INDYCMS	Information + Referral List
INNOPAC@MAINE	Innovative Interfaces Users
INT-LAW@UMINN1	Foreign and International Law Librarians
LABMGR@UKCC	Academic Microcomputer Lab Management
LIBADMIN@UMAB	Library Administration and Management
LIBMASTR@UOTTAWA	Library Master Bibliographic Database
LIBPLN-L@QUCDN	Library Planning
LIBRARY@INDYCMS	Libraries and Librarians
LIBREF-L@KENTVM	Discussion of Library Reference Issues

`LIBRES@KENTVM`	Library and Information Science Research
`MAPS-L@UGA`	Maps and Air Photo Forum
`MEDLIB-L@UBVM`	Medical and Health Sciences Libraries
`MLA-L@IUBVM`	Music Library Association
`MULTILIS@ALBNYVM1`	MULTILIS Users
`NOTIS-L@TCSVM`	NOTIS Users
`NOTISACQ@CUVMB`	NOTIS Acquisitions Discussion Group
`NOTMUS-L@UBVM`	NOTIS Music Library List
`NOTRBCAT@INDYCMS`	Rare Book and Special Collections Catalogers
`NYSO-L@UBVM`	MLA New York State/Ontario Chapter Discussion List
`OFFCAMP@WAYNEST1`	Off-Campus Library Services List
`PACS-L@UHUPVM1`	Public-Access Computer Systems Forum
`PACS-P@UHUPVM1`	PACS-L Publications Only
`SERIALST@UVMVM`	Serials Users Discussion Group
`SPILIB-L@SUVM`	SPIRES Users
`USMARC-L@MAINE`	USMARC Advisory Group Forum
`VTLSLIST@VTVM1`	VTLS Users Discussion Group
`Z3950IW@NERVM`	Z39.50 Implementors Workshop

To subscribe, send the e-mail message:

`SUBSCRIBE List First Name Last Name`

to `LISTSERV@NODE`, where node is the part of the address after the "@" character.

(If you are not on BITNET, ask your computer center how to address a message to the desired BITNET node.)

For example, Jane Doe sends the following e-mail message to `LISTSERV@UHUPVM1` to subscribe to `PACS-L`:

`LIST GLOBAL`

A useful directory of BITNET and Internet conferences, which is classified by subject and includes descriptions, is also available. Send the following commands to `LISTSERV@KENTVM`:

```
GET ACADLIST README
GET ACADLIST FILE1
GET ACADLIST FILE2
GET ACADLIST FILE3
GET ACADLIST FILE4
GET ACADLIST FILE5
GET ACADLIST FILE6
GET ACADLIST FILE7
```

For further information, contact Diane Kovacs: `DKOVACS@KENTVM`.

1.2 Internet Lists

Conservation DistList (Conservation of Archive, Library, and Museum Materials)
> Send a subscription request to Walter Henry: `WHENRY@LINDY.STANFORD.EDU`.

`DYNIX-L@OYSTER.SMCM.EDU` (DYNIX Users)
> Send a subscription request to Todd D. Kelley: `KELLEY@OYSTER.SMCM.EDU`.

`IAMSLIC@UCSD.EDU` (International Association of Aquatic and Marine Science Libraries and Information Centers)
> Send the following command to `LISTSERV@UCSD.EDU`:
> `SUBSCRIBE Your E-Mail Address IAMSLIC`.

`LAW-LIB@UCDAVIS.EDU` (Law Librarians)
> Send subscription requests to: `LAW-REQ@UCDAVIS.EDU`
> Contact Elizabeth St. Goar for technical questions: `ESTGOAR@UCDAVIS.EDU`.

`LIB-HYTELNET@SASK.USASK.CA` (HYTELNET Program)
> Send subscription request to Peter Scott: `SCOTT@SKLIB.USASK.CA`.

`LS2K@CC.UTAH.EDU` (LS/2000 Users Group)
> Send subscription request to: `LS2K-REQUEST@CC.UTAH.EDU`.

PALS-L@KNUTH.MTSU.EDU (PALS System)
Send the following message to
LISTSERV@KNUTH.MTSU.EDU:
SUBSCRIBE PALS-L First Name Last Name.

2.0 Electronic Serials

There are a growing number of library-related electronic journals and newsletters available on BITNET and Internet.

ACQNET (The Acquisitions Librarian's Electronic Network)
Send a subscription request to Christian Boissonnas:
CRI@CORNELLC.

ALCTS NETWORK NEWS (Association for Library Collections and Technical Services)
Send the following message to LISTSERV@UICVM:
SUBSCRIBE ALCTS First Name Last Name. For a list of back issue files, send the message: INDEX ALCTS.

Citations for Serial Literature
Send the following message to LISTSERV@MITVMA:
SUBSCRIBE SERCITES First Name Last Name.

Consortium Update (SPIRES)
Send a subscription request to: HQ.CON@STANFORD.

Current Cites
TELNET MELVYL.UCOP.EDU; Enter command:
SHOW CURRENT CITES (Also distributed on PACS-L.)
Further information: David F. W. Robison,
DROBISON@UCBLIBRA

Hot Off the Tree (HOTT) (Excerpts and Abstracts of Articles about Information Technology)
TELNET MELVYL.UCOP.EDC; Enter command: SHOW HOTT.
Further information: Susan Jurist, SJURIS@UCSD.EDU.

IRLIST Digest (Information Retrieval List Digest)
Send the following message to LISTSERV@UCCVMA:
SUBSCRIBE IR-L First Name Last Name. For a list of back issue files, send the message: INDEX IR-L.

MeckJournal
> Send a subscription request to
> `MECKLER@TIGGER.JVNC.NET`.

Newsletter on Serials Pricing Issues
> Send the following message to `LISTSERV@UNCVX1`:
> `SUBSCRIBE PRICES-L First Name Last Name`

Public-Access Computer Systems News
> Sent to PACS-L and PACS-P subscribers. See above. For
> a list of back issue files, send the following message to
> `LISTSERV@UHUPVM1: INDEX PACS-L`.

The Public-Access Computer Systems Review
> Sent to PACS-L and PACS-P subscribers. See above.
> For a list of article files, send the following message to
> `LISTSERV@UHUPVM1: INDEX PACS-L`.

To obtain a complete list of electronic serials, send the following commands to `LISTSERV@UOTTAWA`:

> `GET EJOURNL1 DIRECTRY`
> `GET EJOURNL2 DIRECTRY`

For further information, contact Michael Strangelove: `441495@ACADVM1.UOTTAWA.CA`.

INDEX

Barbara I. Dewey is currently director of Administrative and Access Services at the University of Iowa Libraries. Prior to her position at Iowa she was director of Admissions and Placement, Indiana University School of Library and Information Science, reference librarian at Northwestern University Library, and head of Reference and Adult Services at the public library in Mankato, Minn. She is the author of *Library Jobs: How to Find Them, How to Fill Them* (Oryx, 1987).

Sheila D. Creth has held the position of university librarian, University of Iowa Libraries, since January 1987. She has held administrative positions in the libraries of the universities of Michigan and Connecticut and Columbia University. Creth holds a master's degree in communication from the University of Connecticut. She has published extensively on organizational and administrative issues related to research libraries. She serves on the Board of Research Libraries Group and is active in the Association of Research Libraries.